MW01517398

Samoa,
A Hundred Years Ago
and Long Before

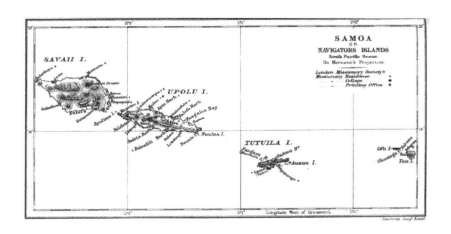

CONTENTS

CHAPTER I.

POSITION OF THE ISLANDS—EARLY VISITORS AND TRADITIONARY ORIGIN.

Samoa is the native name of the group of volcanic islands in central Polynesia long known as the "Navigators Islands." They are situated about 3000 miles from Sydney, and stand on the charts between the parallels of 13° and 15° south latitude, and 168° and 173° west longitude. The mountains of Savaii, one of which is 4000 feet high, may be seen 50 miles off, and, on coming near, the stranger finds a lovely island, 150 miles in circumference, and covered with vegetation as far as the eye can reach. The mountains of Upolu and Tutuila rise 2000 and 3000 feet above the level of the sea, and present the same aspect of richness and fertility. These are the principal islands of the group. They run east and west. Upolu, 130 miles in circumference, is in the middle, having Savaii 10 miles to the west; and Tutuila, an island 80 miles in circumference, about 40 miles to the east. There are several smaller islands which are inhabited, and several other isolated romantic spots here and there which are not inhabited.

Upolu is almost entirely surrounded by barrier reefs: these wonderful submarine walls, or breakwaters, built up to the level of the sea and forming a fine smooth lagoon, invaluable for fishing and facilitating all kinds of communication between the settlements along the coast. The distance between the shore and the reef is from thirty feet to three or four miles. In some places the lagoons are shallow, and require the rise of the tide to allow a canoe or boat to pass along; in other places, and particularly where there are openings in the reef, they are from ten to twenty fathoms deep, and afford anchorage to ships. The rivers are neither numerous nor large, but there is no lack of fresh water; it springs up in abundance in many parts in the interior and along the coast.

The Dutch "three-ship expedition," under Roggewein, in 1722, seems to have been the first to notice these islands. Then followed the French navigators, Bougainville and La Perouse, the former in 1768 and the latter in 1787. Bougainville, seeing the natives move about so much in canoes, gave the group the name of the "Isles of the Navigators." Captain Cook heard of them in 1773 from the Tongans, noted some of their names, and in 1791 they were visited by H.B.M. ship *Pandora*. Little, however, was known of these islands until 1830, when a mission was commenced there by the agents of the London Missionary Society.

The natives, who number about 35,000, are of the prevailing light copper colour of central and eastern Polynesia. Hardly a vestige is to be seen among them of the crisped and woolly-haired dark-brown Papuans, or western Polynesian negroes. But as the physical characteristics and languages of central and eastern Polynesia are well known, I pass on to other and traditionary matters, and begin with what the Samoans have to say on COSMOGONY AND MAN.

1. There was first of all Leai, *nothing*. Thence sprung Nanamu, *fragrance*. Then Efuefu, *dust*. Then Iloa, *perceivable*. Then Maua, *obtainable*. Then Eleele, *earth*. Then Papatu, *high rocks*. Then Maataanoa, *small stones*. Then Maunga, *mountains*. Then Maunga married Malaeliua, or changeable meeting-place, and had a daughter called Fasiefu, *piece of dust*. She married Lave i fulufulu tolo, or down of the sugar-cane flower, and to her was born three sons: Mua, *first*; Uso, *brother*; Talu, and their sister Sulitonu, or true heir. And then follows a story as to Mua and Talu originating the names of two districts on the island of Upolu.

2. A cosmical genealogy takes the form of married couples, and runs as follows:—

	Male	Female	Progeny
1.	The high rocks.	The earth rocks.	The earth.
2.	The earth.	High winds.	Solid clouds.
3.	Solid clouds.	Flying clouds.	(1) Confused winds. (2) Quiet winds. (3) Boisterous winds. (4) Land beating winds. (5) Dew of life.
4.	Dew of life.	Clouds clinging to the heavens.	Clouds flying about.
5.	Clouds flying about.	Clear heavens.	(1) Shadow. (2) Twilight. (3) Daylight. (4) Noonday. (5) Afternoon. (6) Sunset.
6.	Quiet winds.	Beautiful clouds.	Cloudless heavens.
7.	Cloudless	Spread out	Tangaloa the heavens. heavens. originator of men.
8.	Tangaloa	Great heavens.	Tangaloa of the heavens.
9.	Tangaloa of the heavens.	Keeper of the heavens.	Pili.
10.	Pili.	Sina the tropic bird.	(1) Sanga. (2) Ana. (3) Tua. (4) Tolufale. (5) Muganitama.
11.	Ana.	Sina the powerful.	Matofaana.
12.	Matofaana.	Sina the bald.	Veta.
13.	Veta.	Afu lilo.	Naituveta.
14.	Naituveta.	Toe lauoo.	Toso.

15.	Toso.	Langi fiti pula.	Siu tau lalovasa.
16.	Siu tau lalovasa.	Pai (who reckoned the light).	Siu toso.
17.	Siu toso.	Lau lano ma lau vai.	Ata.
18.	Ata.	Uliaumi.	Siufeai.
19.	Siufeai.	Polaitu.	Siu le lau mato.
20.	Siu le lau mato.	Sina i lau tolo.	Feepo.
21.	Feepo.	Sea faetele.	Ationgie.
22.	Ationgie.	Tau vai upolu.	Savea.

This Savea was the first Malietoa, and then in the continuance of this genealogy there follow twenty-three generations of Malietoa, down to Malietoa Talavou, who was proclaimed king in 1878, and subsequently recognised by the Governments of England, Germany, and the United States. Many other traditionary genealogies of chiefs might be given, but let the above suffice as a specimen of the rest.

3. Other descendants of Cloudless heavens (No. 6 above):—

	Male.	*Female.*	*Progeny.*
(1)	Cloudless heavens.	The eighth heavens.	Tangaloa the dweller in lands.
(2)	Tangaloa dweller in lands.	Cloudy heavens.	Tangaloa the explorer of lands.
(3)	Tangaloa the explorer of lands.	Queen of earth.	Valevalenoa, or *space*.

Space had a long-legged seat. At another birth Cloudy heavens brought forth a head. This was the head that was said to have fallen from the heavens. Space set it up on his high stool and said to it, "O beloved! be a son—be a second with me on the earth." Space started back, for all of a sudden the body of a man-child was added to the head. The child was sensible, and inquired who his father was. Space replied, "Your father is yonder in the East, yonder in the West, yonder towards the sea, and yonder in-land, yonder above and yonder below." Then the boy said, "I have found my name, call me All the sides of heaven." And from him sprang the four divisions, East, West, North, and South. He grew up to manhood, went to the North, married and had children. Went to the South, married and had children. Went to the East, married and had children. Went to the West, married and had children. He then went up to the heavens, and told all his children to follow him.

4. The children of Ilu, *worm*, and Mamao, *distant*, were:—

  (1)   Papa tu, or great rocks.
  (2)   Papa one, or sandy rocks.
  (3)   Papa ele, or earthy rocks.
  (4)   Masina, or the moon.
  (5)   La, or the sun.
  (6)   Sami, or the sea.
  (7)   Vai, or fresh water.

These were all sons, and then there were two daughters, the one named Great wind and the other Gentle wind.

They all separated and lived apart, but the sea was shut up. Then the children said, "Let the sea be set free and allowed to come out that we may look at it." This was done, and then the three kinds of rocks were flooded and died, but the sun and the moon fled to the heavens and lived.

5. Fire and water married, and from them sprung the earth, rocks, trees, and everything.

The cuttle-fish fought with the fire and was beaten. The fire fought with the rocks, and the rocks conquered. The large stones fought with the small ones; the small conquered. The small stones fought with the grass, and the grass conquered. The grass fought with the trees; the grass was beaten and the trees conquered. The trees fought with the creepers, the trees were beaten and the creepers conquered. The creepers rotted, swarmed with maggots, and from maggots they grew to be men.

6.   The god Tangaloa existed in space, but we do not know how or whence he came. He wished some place to live in, and so he made the heavens. He also wished to have a place under the heavens, and so he made the Lalolangi, *under the heavens*, or the earth. Savaii was formed by a stone rolled down from the heavens, Upolu by another. Other stories say that they were drawn up from under the ocean by a fishing-hook. He next made the Fee or cuttle-fish, and told it to go down under the earth, and hence the lower regions of sea or land are called Sa le feé, or sacred to the cuttle-fish. The cuttle-fish brought forth all kinds of rocks, and hence the great one on which we live.

7.   Tangaloa the god of heaven sent down his daughter in the form of the bird Turî, a species of snipe, *Charadrius fulvus*. She flew about, but could find no resting-place, nothing but ocean. She returned to the heavens, but was again sent down by Tangaloa to search for land. First she observed spray, then lumpy places, then water breaking, then land above the surface, and then a dry place where she could rest. She went back and told her father. He again sent her down; she reported extending surface of land, and then he sent her down with some earth and a creeping plant. The plant grew, and she continued to come down and visit it. After a time its leaves withered. On her next visit it was swarming with worms or maggots, and the next time she came down they had become men and women.

8.   The ants and the small coral made the small stones. The small and large stones caused the loose rocks, and from the loose rocks and the fire sprang a man called Ariari, *to appear*, and from him and a woman sprang the cuttle-fish and the race of men.

9. Man is formed from a species of mussel. If made of the hard mussel he lives long—it is difficult for him to die. But if he happens to be made of the poisonous mussel, he is fragile, easily upset, and does not live long.

The soul of man is called his angânga, or that which goes or comes. It is said to be the daughter of Taufanuu, or *vapour of lands*, which forms clouds, and as the dark cloudy covering of night comes on, man feels sleepy, because his soul wishes to go and visit its mother.

10. All the gods had a meeting at a public place on Upolu to decide what was to be the end of the life of man. One god made a speech and proposed that it should be like the extinction of the cocoa-nut-leaf torch, which when it goes out can be shaken, blown, and blaze up again, so that man after sickness and death might rise again in all the vigour of youth.

Another god called the Supa or *paralysis*, rose and proposed that the life of man should be like the extinction of the candle-nut torch, which when once out cannot be blown in again.

Then followed a number of speeches, some for the one proposal and some for the other. While the discussion was proceeding a pouring rain came on and broke up the meeting. The gods ran to the houses for shelter, and as they were dispersing they called out, "Let the proposal of Paralysis be carried, and let man's life go out like the candle-nut torch." And hence the proverb: "It is as Paralysis said." Man dies and does not return.

Another account of this meeting adds other two proposals. One that men should cast their skins like the shell-fish; and another that when they grow old they should dive in the "water of life" and come up little boys. It finishes, however, with the proposal of Paralysis being carried, but adds that only men were to die, not women.

CHAPTER II.

SAMOA.—*ORIGIN OF THE NAME.*

1. The rocks married the earth, and the earth became pregnant. Salevao, the god of the rocks, observed motion in the moa or *centre* of the earth. The child was born and named Moa, from the place where it was seen moving. Salevao ordered the umbilicus to be laid on a club, and cut with a stone; and hence the custom ever after on the birth of a man-child.

    Salevao then provided water for washing the child and made it sa, or *sacred* to Moa. The rocks and the earth said they wished to get some of that water to drink. Salevao replied that if they got a bamboo he would send them a streamlet through it, and hence the origin of springs.

    Salevao said he would become loose stones, and that everything which grew would be sa ia Moa, or *sacred to* Moa, till his hair was cut. After a time his hair was cut and the restriction taken off, and hence also the rocks and the earth were called Sa ia Moa, or as it is abbreviated, SAMOA.

2. Tangaloa of the heavens had two children—a son called *Moa*, and a daughter called Lu. Lu married a brother chief of Tangaloa, and had a son, who was named Lu after herself. One night when Tangaloa lay down to sleep, he heard his grandson singing—

    Moa Lu,

Moa Lu.

After a time he changed it to—

Lu Moa,
Lu Moa.

Tangaloa was annoyed at the presumption of the lad, as if he wished to be above Moa the firstborn. He feigned an errand, and called the boy to come and scratch his back. The boy went to perform the operation, but on stretching out his hand was seized by his grandfather, and beaten with the handle of his fly-flapper. Lu made his escape, came running down to the earth, and named it SAMOA.

3. At one time the land was flooded by the sea, and everything died except some fowls and pigeons. The pigeons flew away, but the Moa, or *fowls*, remained and were made sacred by Lu, and not to be killed, and hence called the Sa Moa or *preserve fowls* of Lu.
4. Tangaloa of the heavens and his son Lu built a canoe or vessel up in the heavens. They were aided by a carpenter called Manufili. When finished it was taken down and set on the Laueleele, or surface of the earth. There was no sea at that time.

Lu had a wife called Gaogao o le tai, *expanse of sea*. She had a son who was also called Lu, and when he grew up the vessel was given to him. When she next brought forth it was a lot of all kinds of shell-fish. Lu said to his mother, "What is the use of having all these things lying there bare in the sun?" "Leave it with me to make a *lake* for them," was her reply; and then she told him to go and get his vessel in order, and be ready to get into it when the sea was made.

The sea was the product of the next birth. Lu caught two fowls, and when the sea rose took them with him into the vessel. He was not many days afloat, some say six, when his vessel rested on the top of the mountain called Malata, in Atua, east end of Upolu. Lu lived there at the village called Uafato, and had there his Sa Moa, or *preserve fowls*, which were not to be killed. Another story says that Lu came from the west with his fowls, and that from his crew all the islands of the group were peopled. He was said to have come from Pulotu, Papatea, Pau, Vau, Aoao, and Ngaelu. Others say he came with his fowls direct from Tafiti apaau, or the *Winged Fiji*.

Two of the people of Tangaloa of the heavens came down to fish. As they were returning with two baskets of fish, the fowls of Lu leaped up to peck at the fish. The lads caught and killed the precious preserve, or Sa Moa, and ran off with them to the heavens.

In the morning Lu missed the fowls, and went off in search of them. He saw from the unbroken early morning cobwebs across the roads east and west, that no one had passed along there. He suspected the fishing party from the heavens, and away he went up there from the top of the mountain. He had nothing in his hand but his fly-flapper.

In the first heavens he smelled roast fowl, and presently he came upon the two culprits as they were eating, and believed that they were crunching the bones of the very fowls of which he was in search. He charged them. They did not deny, but commenced to lay the blame the one on the other, and hence the proverb to this day: "It was not I, but you." He set upon both of them with his fue, or fly-flapper, and hence the word to *fue*, or to fly-flapper, is used as a milder term to express beating or killing.

Away the lads fled, and he after them up through the nine heavens, laying out on them with his fue. When they reached the tenth heaven, Tangaloa made his appearance and called out, "What is all this about? Don't you know this is Malae totoa, the *place of rest?* There must be no fighting here."

In the tenth heaven no strife was allowed; the place was kept beautifully clean, no rubbish to be seen about the roads, and there were no clubs hanging in the houses.

Lu told the cause of his anger: his Sa Moa or preserve fowls had been stolen, and he had found the thieves in the very act of eating them. Tangaloa said, "It is indeed very bad; but now that you have left behind all the places where wars may be fought out, and have come to this heaven of peace, let your wrath abate, spare these men, and you shall go back with the title of *King of heaven*, and take my daughter Langituavalu, *Eighth heavens*, to be your wife." "Very good," said Lu; "let these men live, and let us be at peace, and conform to the custom of Malae totoa."

A handsome dowry was got up, the marriage took place, and Tangaloa told Lu to name the earth Samoa when he came down, and so keep in remembrance his *preserve fowls*.

The two came down, had a child, and named him Samoa, and from them these islands have been peopled. Hence also the proverb from this lady coming from heaven and having children on earth: "The heavens are swinging and touching the earth." Of any one who marries a person far away it is also said, "It is like Langituavalu."

At the marriage of Langituavalu and Lu, Tangaloa ordered all his people to contribute a fine white mat each, with which to form her dowry. A great feast was also provided, but only those were admitted who had contributed a white mat. When the festive day came there were many outside who were chagrined that they had not made an effort to get the white mat, and so have been permitted to share in the grand celebration, to the music of which they could only listen outside and in the distance.

CHAPTER III.

A FUTURE STATE—RELIGION, ETC.

The Samoans believed in a soul or disembodied spirit, which they called the *angânga*. Anga means to *go* or *come*, according to the particle of direction suffixed. Anga *atu* means to go away; anga *mai* signifies to come. The reduplicated angânga is used to designate the soul as distinct from the body, and which at death was supposed to go away from the body and proceed to the hadean regions under the ocean, which they called Pulotu.

In describing the localities about Falealupo in another chapter, we have noted some things about the lower regions which were supposed to enter from the neighbourhood of Falealupo. We know little, if anything, more of the notions which the Samoans had of a future state, and therefore pass on to the religion which prevailed all over the group.

At one time it was supposed that Samoa was destitute of any kind of religion, and by some of the early visitors the people were called "the *godless* Samoans." On closer acquaintance with them, however, it was discovered that they lived under the influence of a host of imaginary deities, claiming alike belief and corresponding practice.

At his birth a Samoan was supposed to be taken under the care of some god, or *aitu*, as it was called. The help of several of these gods was probably invoked in succession on the occasion, and the one who happened to be addressed just as the child was born was fixed on as the child's god for life.

These gods were supposed to appear in some *visible incarnation*, and the particular thing in which his god was in the habit of appearing was to the Samoan an object of veneration. It was, in fact, his idol, and he was careful never to injure it or treat it with contempt. One, for instance, saw his god in the eel, another in the shark, another in the turtle, another in the dog, another in the owl, another in the lizard, and so on throughout all the fish of the sea, and birds, and four-footed beasts, and creeping things. In some of the shell-fish, even, gods were supposed to be present. A man would eat freely of what was regarded as the incarnation of the god of another man, but the incarnation of his own particular god he would consider it death to injure or to eat. The god was supposed to avenge the insult by taking up his abode in that person's body, and causing to generate there the very thing which he had eaten, until it produced death. This class of genii, or tutelary deities, they called *aitu fale*, or gods of the house.

The father of the family was *the high-priest*, and usually offered a short prayer at the evening meal, that they might all be kept from fines, sickness, war, and death. Occasionally, too, he would direct that they have a family feast in honour of their household gods; and on these occasions a cup of their intoxicating ava draught was poured out as a drink-offering. They did this in their family house, where they were all assembled, supposing that their gods had a spiritual presence there, as well as in the material objects to which we have referred. Often it was supposed that the god came among them, and spoke through the father or some other member of the family, telling them what to do in order to remove a present evil or avert a threatened one. Sometimes it would be that the family should get a canoe built and keep it sacred to the god. They might travel in it and use it themselves, but it was death to sell or part with a canoe which had been built specially for the god.

Another class of Samoan deities may be called gods of the town or village. Every village had its god, and every one born in that village was regarded as the property of that god. I have got a child for so-and-so, a woman would say on the birth of her child, and name the village god. There was a small house or temple also consecrated to the deity of the place. Where there was no formal temple, the great house of the village, where the chiefs were in the habit of assembling, was the temple for the time being, as occasion required. Some settlements had a sacred grove as well as a temple, where prayers and offerings were presented.

In their temples they had generally something for the eye to rest upon with superstitious veneration. In one might be seen a conch shell, suspended from the roof in a basket made of cinnet network; and this the god was supposed to blow when he wished the people to rise to war. In another, two stones were kept. In another, something resembling the head of a man, with white streamers flying, was raised on a pole at the door of the temple, on the usual day of worship. In another, a cocoa-nut shell drinking-cup was suspended from the roof, and before it prayers were addressed and offerings presented. This cup was also used in oaths. If they wished to find out a thief, the suspected parties were assembled before the chiefs, the cup sent for, and each would approach, lay his hand on it, and say, "With my hand on this cup, may the god look upon me, and send swift destruction, if I took the thing which has been stolen." The stones and the shells were used in a similar way. Before this ordeal, the truth was rarely concealed. They firmly believed that it would be death to touch the cup and tell a lie.

The priests in some cases were the chiefs of the place; but in general some one in a particular family claimed the privilege, and professed to declare the will of the god. His office was hereditary. He fixed the days for the annual feasts in honour of the deity, received the offerings, and thanked the people for them. He decided also whether or not the people might go to war.

The offerings were principally cooked food. The first cup was in honour of the god. It was either poured out on the ground or *waved* towards the heavens. The chiefs all drank a portion out of the same cup, according to rank; and after that the food brought as an offering was divided and eaten there before the god. This feast was annual, and frequently about the month of May. In some places it passed off quietly; in others it was associated with games, sham-fights, night-dances, etc., and lasted for days. In time of war special feasts were ordered by the priests. Of the offerings on war occasions women and children were forbidden to partake, as it was not their province to go to battle. They supposed it would bring sickness and death on the party eating who did not go to the war, and hence were careful to bury or throw into the sea whatever food was over after the festival. In some cases the feasts in honour of the god were regulated by the appearance in the settlement of the bird which was thought to be the incarnation of the god. Whenever the bird was seen the priest would say that the god had come, and fix upon a day for his entertainment.

The village gods, like those of the household, had all some particular incarnation: one was supposed to appear as a bat, another as a heron, another as an owl. If a man found a dead owl by the roadside, and if that happened to be the incarnation of his village god, he would sit down and weep over it, and beat his forehead with stones till the blood flowed. This was thought pleasing to the deity. Then the bird would be wrapped up and buried with care and ceremony, as if it were a human body. This, however, was not the death of the god. He was supposed to be yet alive, and incarnate in all the owls in existence. The flight of these birds was observed in time of war. If the bird flew before them, it was a signal to go on; but if it crossed the path, it was a bad omen, and a sign to retreat. Others saw their village god in the rainbow, others saw him in the shooting star; and in time of war the position of a rainbow and the direction of a shooting star were always ominous.

The constant dread of the gods, and the numerous and extravagant demands of a cunning and avaricious priesthood, made the heathenism of Samoa a hard service.

I have collected and arranged alphabetically in the two following chapters the names of the principal gods formerly worshipped in Samoa. The notices of each will explain more fully the religion of the people, and especially that system of zoolatry which so extensively prevailed.

CHAPTER IV.

GODS SUPERIOR—
WAR AND GENERAL VILLAGE GODS.

1. AITU LANGI, or *Gods of heaven.*

1. These gods were supposed to have fallen from the heavens at the call of a blind man to protect his son from a cannibal chief. They were scattered over several villages, but did not move about in the bodies of mortals. A large temple was erected to one of them in which there were ten seats on which sat the principal chiefs. A large shell was the only visible representation of the god, and in time of war it was carefully consulted. If it stood on end and made an unusual noise they went to battle cheerfully; if, however, it only murmured what they imagined to be "Go back, go back," there was no fighting that day. Tupai was the name of the high priest and prophet. He was greatly dreaded. His very look was poison. If he looked at a cocoa-nut tree it died, and if he glanced at a bread-fruit tree it also withered away.

2. Aitu langi was the name of a village god in another place, and supposed to be incarnate in the owl. If, when going to fight, an owl flew before, it was a good sign; but if across the road or backwards they returned immediately.

2. ALII TU, or *The God who stands.*

This god was seen in the Ve'a, or rail (*Raltus pectoralis*). The flight of this bird was also observed during war. If it flew before, it was a good omen; if otherwise they went back disconcerted.

3. AVE I LE TALA, Or *Take to the end of the house.*

This was the name of an accoucheur god, whose priest went, when sent for, and prayed for the safety of the patient. This god is specially noted as having predicted the arrival of a powerful foreign god, who was to eat up all the gods of Samoa except one, and that was himself; and then he added pathetically through the priest to the family where he was supposed to reside, "When the great god comes, do not you all leave me, but let two still keep aloof and stand by me." On the introduction and rapid spread of Christianity many said, "The prediction of Ave i le tala has come true."

4. FONGE AND TOAFA.

1. These were the names of two oblong smooth stones which stood on a raised platform of loose stones inland of one of the villages. They were supposed to be the parents of Saato, a god who controlled the rain. When the chiefs and people were ready to go off for weeks to certain places in the bush for the sport of pigeon-catching, offerings of cooked taro and fish were laid on the stones, accompanied by prayers for fine weather and no rain. Any one who refused an offering to the stones was frowned upon; and in the event of rain was blamed and punished for bringing down the wrath of the fine-weather god, and spoiling the sports of the season.
2. Persons going to search for bush yams in time of scarcity gave a yam to the stones as a thank-offering, supposing that these gods caused

the yams to grow, and could lead them to the best places for finding such edible roots.

3. Any one passing by casually with a basket of cooked food would stop and lay a morsel on the stones.

4. When such offerings were eaten in the night by dogs or rats, it was supposed that the god chose to become incarnate for the time being in the form of such living creatures.

5. Fanonga, *Destruction.*

1. This was the name of a war-god, and supposed to be incarnate in the Samoan owl (*Strix delicatula*). In time of war, offerings of food were presented to a pet one which was kept for the purpose. If it flew about above while the troops were walking along below that was a good omen; but if it flew away in the direction of the enemy it was supposed to have left the one party and gone to join the other, and therefore a calamity.

2. At the beginning of the annual fish festivals, the chiefs and people of the village assembled round the opening of the first oven, and give the first fish to the god.

3. A dead owl found under a tree in the settlement was the signal for all the village to assemble at the place, burn their bodies with firebrands, and beat their foreheads with stones till the blood flowed, and so they expressed their sympathy and condolence with the god over the calamity "by an offering of blood." He still lived, however, and moved about in all the other existing owls of the country.

6. Faamalu, *Shade.*

1. The name of a village god, and represented by a trumpet-shell. On the month for annual worship all the people met in the place of public gatherings with heaps of cooked food. First there were offerings

and prayers to the god to avert calamities and give prosperity; then they feasted with and before their god, and after that any strangers present might eat.

At the same settlement a marine deity called Tamauanuu, or *Plenty for the land*, was worshipped at the same time. On that day no one dared to swim on his back off the settlement, or eat a cocoa-nut. Any one transgressing would have to go to the beach and beat his forehead with stones till the blood flowed, so as to prevent his being devoured by a shark the next time he went to fish.

In time of war Faamalu was also represented by a fish, the movements of which were watched. If it was seen to swim briskly they went to battle cheerfully; but if it turned round now and then on its back that was a veto on fighting.

Faamalu was also seen in a cloud or shade. If a cloud preceded them in going to battle they advanced courageously; if, however, the clouds were all behind they were afraid.

2. In a quarrel a mischief-maker would be cursed and given over to the wrath of Faamalu. If anything was stolen the sufferer would go along the road shouting and calling on Faamalu to be avenged on the thief.
3. In another district Faamalu was only a war-god—had a temple with a shell in it, and the shell was carried about with the troops. The trees all around the temple were sacred, and never used for any purpose.

7. FAAOLA, *Life-giver.*

The name of a war-god. Before going to fight the people of the district where he was worshipped all met and prayed that they might be "strong-hearted" and free from cowardice.

8. O Le Fe'e, *The cuttle-fish (Octopus).*

1. This was a war-god said to have been brought by a chief called Tapuaau, who swam hither from Fiji with his cuttle-fish. When taken into a house it showed a special fondness for a piece of white native cloth by stretching over to it, and hence this white cloth became an emblem of the god, and his worshippers in going to battle were known by white turbans, which they thought would please the god and be a defence against the enemy.

Before starting all assembled in the public place of the village, and one of the priests prayed as follows:—

> Le Fe'e e! faafofoga mai ia
> O au o Fale le a tulai atu nei.
> Le Fe'e e! au mai ia ou mŭmŭ fua
> Sei tau a'i le taua nei.

Which may be translated as follows:—O Fe'e! listen—I am Fale who now stand up—O Fe'e! give us your red flaming rage with which to fight this battle.

All listened carefully to the enunciation of this prayer by the priest, for if he was observed to *stutter* in a single word it was a bad omen.

The Fe'e was also supposed to be present in the white shell of the *Cypræa ovula*; hence a string of these shells was suspended in the house of the priest, and were supposed to murmur, or "cry," when war was determined on. The colour of the shells was also watched. A clear white was a good omen, but if they looked dark and dingy it was a bad one.

The movements of the cuttle-fish at sea were also looked after at war-times. If seen near the shore when the people were mustering for battle it was a good sign; if far off the reverse.

2. In one place the Fe'e was a general village god, whose province was not confined to war. The month of May was sacred to his worship. No traveller was then allowed to pass through the village by the public road; nor was any canoe allowed in the lagoon off that part of the settlement. There was great feasting, too, on these occasions, and also games, club exercise, spear-throwing, wrestling, etc.

A new temple was at this time erected, to the material of which every man, woman, and child contributed something, even if only a stick or a reed of thatch. Some were drafted off to put up the house, and the rest commenced to fight in real earnest, and settle any old grudges with each other. He who got the most wounds was set down for special favours from the god. With the completion of the temple the fighting ended, and that was to suffice for the year. A quarrel of neighbours at any other time, and rising to blows, was frowned upon by the god Fe'e, because it was not left till next year and temple-building day.

In another district three months were sacred to the worship of the Fe'e. During that time any one passing along the road, or in the lagoon, would be beaten, if not killed, for insulting the god. For the first month torches and all other lights were forbidden, as the god was about and did not wish to be seen. White turbans were also forbidden during the festivities, and confined to war. At this time, also, all unsightly projecting burdens—such as a log of firewood on the shoulder—were forbidden, lest it should be considered by the god as a mockery of his *tentacula*.

The priest at this place had a large wooden bowl, which he called lipi, or *sudden death*. This was another representative of the god, and by this the family had no small gains. In a case of stealing, fine mats or other gifts were taken by the injured party to the priest to curse the thief and make him ill. The priest would then sit down with some select members of the family around the bowl representative of the god, and pray for speedy vengeance on the guilty; then they waited the issue. These imprecations were dreaded. Conscience-stricken thieves, when taken ill, were carried off by their friends on a litter and laid down at the door of the priest, with taro, cocoa-nuts, or yams, in lieu of those confessed to have been stolen; and they would add fine mats and other presents, that the priest might pray again over the death-bowl, and have the sentence reversed.

There is a story that the cuttle-fish gods of Savaii were once chased by an Upolu hero, who caught them in a great net and killed them. They were changed into stones, and now stand up in a rocky part of the lagoon on the north side of Upolu. For a long time travelling parties from Savaii felt *eerie* when they came to the place—did not like to go through between the stones, but took the outside passage.

Another fragment makes out that a Savaii Fe'e married the daughter of a chief on Upolu, and for convenience in coming and going made a hole in the reef, and hence the harbour at Apia. He went up the river also at that place, and built a stone house inland, the "Stonehenge" relics of which are still pointed out, and named to this day "the house of the Fe'e." In time of war he sent a branch drifting down the river as a good omen, and a sign to the people that they might go on with the war, sure of driving the enemy.

3. In some instances the Fe'e was a household god only. If any visitor caught a cuttle-fish and cooked it, or if any member of that family had been where a cuttle-fish was eaten, the family would meet over the case, and a man or woman would be selected to go and lie down in a *cold* oven, and be covered over with leaves, as in the process of baking, and all this as a would-be or mock burnt-offering to avert the wrath of the god. While this was being done the family united in praying: "O bald-headed Fe'e! forgive what has been done—it was all the work of a *stranger*." Failing such signs of respect and humility, it was supposed the god would come to the family, and cause a cuttle-fish to grow internally, and be the death of some of them.

9. Fuai Langi, *Beginner of the Heavens.*

A god of one of the small islands, and seen in the sea-eel, or *Marœna*. If the sea-eel happened to be driven on to the shore in a gale or by any tidal wave it portended evil, and created a commotion all over the place.

10. Ga'e Fefe, *Breathless fear.*

A war-god in some of the villages, and seen in a cocoa-nut-leaf basket. It is said that during a battle between the gods of Samoa and those of Tonga the former crouched about the trunks of the cocoa-nut trees; but Ga'e fefe hid in a cocoa-nut-leaf basket, and escaped while many others were killed. Hence the *basket* became a sign of the god, and no one would step over such a thing, supposing the god might be in it. Hence, also, if in going to fight they fell in with a newly-plaited cocoa-nut-leaf basket turned upside down it was a bad omen, and sent them back. If, however, the basket was an old one, and not lying *across* the road, but to the one side, and "fore and aft," it was a good sign, and encouraged them to proceed.

11. La'ala'a—*Step over*

1. A village war god in Savaii. Supposed to go before the troops, but invisible. When the people turned out, according to hospitality usage, to take food to a travelling party, they would arrange to lay down ten pigs. If the visitors, in recounting and shouting out in public, as they do, what they had got, said that there were *eleven* pigs, it was supposed that the god had added *one.* Then they would compare notes, and say: "Oh yes, it must have been that old woman we saw with a dry shrunk leaf girdle." There were other instances of the "devil's dozen" in Samoa.

Once, when the people were driven by a war fleet from Upolu, the god became incarnate in a *yellow* man, went and lay down in a house, and there they killed him to please the Upolu people and stop the war, which the latter agreed to do in return for killing the god. Out of respect to the god the people of that village never used the word la'ala'a for *stepping over*, but sought a new word in soposopo, which is still a current synonym for la'ala'a.

2. La'ala'a was also the name of a god who took care of the plantations. He guarded them by the help of the god *thunder*. They never spoke of *lightning* as doing harm, it is always the thunder. "Thunder" once struck the house of Fala and Paongo. The family rose up, caught him, tied him up with pandanus leaves, and frightened him by poking him with firebrands. He cried out in distress:

    "Oh! Fala, I'm burning,
    Oh! Paongo, I wish to live!"

They decided to spare him, and make him a god to keep the rats away from their food. They made a hieroglyphic scare for him, also, of a basket filled with pandanus leaves and charred firebrands, and hung it up among the trees, that he might know what to expect if he destroyed a house again. This basket was also a scare for a thief, and an imprecation that *thunder* might destroy his plantation.

3. La'ala'a was also the name of a god in Upolu, who was the champion of *wrestlers*. The place was supposed to be filled with gods who came to wrestle.
4. The same name was given to a god who predicted in war, sickness, and family events. In sickness the people of the village confessed crimes, and prayed that they might be *stepped over* or forgiven. He was

supposed to dwell in the mountain, and any part of it sufficed as a confessional.

There was a priest also who, when he prayed to la'ala'a, became possessed, told the cause of disease, and forbade the evil conduct of the suffering culprit.

12. LAA MAOMAO—*The great step.*

This is one of the names of the rainbow, which was a representative of a war god of several villages. If, when going to battle, a rainbow sprang up right before them and *across* the path, or across the course of the canoes at sea, the troops and the fleet would return. The same if the rainbow arch, or *long step*, of the god was seen behind them. If, however, it was sideways they went on with spirit, thinking the god was marching along with them and encouraging them to advance.

13. MAO MA ULI—*Mistake and Black.*

Two teeth of the sperm whale, and said to have come from Fiji, were so named, and represented the war gods of a large village. They were kept in a cave, and when the people went to fight a priest remained behind to pray for success and watch and report the position of the teeth. If they lay east and west it was a good omen, but if they turned over and lay north and south it was a sign of defeat.

14. MATUU—*Heron,* or *"Andrea sacra."*

The heron was the incarnation of a war god on the island of Manono. If it flew *before* the troops that was a good sign, but the reverse if it flew across the path.

A story is told of Heron and his brother Destruction. They cooked some food one day, but it was not half done. The enraged family set upon the two. Destruction had his neck broken by a stick thrown at him; but Heron escaped by having his neck pulled long, as it is to this day.

15. Moso.

1. This was the name of one of the great *land* gods, in opposition to Tangaloa, the god of the heavens. The root of the word is the name of a tree—"*Cananga odorata*"—the yellow flowers of which are highly fragrant. A stone was his representative in one village, on which passing travellers laid down a scented wreath or necklace as an offering to Moso.

2. In another place Moso's representative was a large wooden bowl, decorated with white shells, and called Lipi, or sudden death, as described under Le Fe'e, No. 8. The priest received offerings from the injured, and, in lieu of them, prayed to Moso with loud crying and forced tears to curse with sudden death the unknown thief or other injurer. "Oh Moso! make haste, show your power, send down to the lower regions, sweep away like a flood, may they never see the light of another day." These were the usual imprecations shrieked out over the bowl.

3. One of the kings of the district of Atua was supposed to be a man and move about among mortals in the daytime; but at night he was Moso, and away among the gods.

4. Moso was also a household god in some families. In one he was incarnate as a man. He helped himself to food of any kind from the plantations of his neighbours, and, if chased, suddenly disappeared; and hence they considered he was a god, and prayed to him and laid down offerings.

5. In another family Moso was said to appear, but only one old man could discern him when he came. A visit was known by the old

man shouting out, "Your excellency! Your excellency has come!" and some such chief's language. Then would follow a conversation between the old man and the god, all through the lips of the old impostor himself; and then the family would hear of some new house, or canoe, or food, or marriage, or something else that was wanted.

6. Moso also appeared in one family in the form of a pet pigeon called the Tu (*Phlegoenas Stairi*). When food was brought in, no water was to be spilled on the doorstep. It would make the protecting god Tu angry, and cause him to go off.

In another family he was incarnate in the domestic fowl, and if any of them ate a piece of fowl the consequence was delirium and death.

In another family Moso was incarnate in the cuttle-fish, and none of them dared to eat one.

Another family had Moso incarnate with them in a creeper bird called the Fuia (*Sturnoides atrifusca*). If it came about in the morning or the evening it was a sign that their prayers were accepted. If it did not come Moso was supposed to be angry. The bird did not appear at noon owing to the glare of the sun. The priest interpreted to the family the meaning of the *chirps* as his inclination or fancy dictated

7. *Long Moso* was the name of another family god. The turtle and the mullet were sacred to him, and eaten only by the priest. The family prayed to him before the evening meal.

8. The Fai, or stinging ray fish, and also the mullet were incarnations of *Moso the strong* in another family. If visitors or friends caught or brought with them either of these fish, a child of the family would be taken and laid down in an unheated oven, as a peace-offering to Moso for the indignity done to him by the strangers. If any member of the family tasted of these sacred fish he was sentenced by the heads

of the family to drink a cupful of rancid oil dregs as a punishment and to stay the wrath of Moso.

16. NAFANUA—*Hidden inland.*

This was the name of the goddess of a district in the west end of the island of Savaii. She was the daughter of Saveasiuleo, the god of Pulotu, and was *hidden* inland, or in the bush, when an infant by her mother, who was ashamed of the illegitimate birth. She came from Pulotu, the Samoan haedes, at a time when the ruling power was so oppressive as to compel the people to climb cocoa-nut trees with their feet upwards, their heads downwards, and to pluck the nuts with their toes. As she passed along she saw a poor fellow struggling up a tree with his head downward, and calling out in despair that he could endure it no longer. She told him to come down, and that she would put an end to it. She summoned all to battle, took the lead herself, and completely routed the enemy, and raised the district to a position of honour and equality. When she went to the fight she covered her breasts with cocoa-nut leaflets that the enemy might not see she was a woman, and the distinguishing mark or pass-word of her troops was a few cocoa-nut leaflets bound round the waist. After the battle in which she conquered, she ordered cocoa-nut leaflets to be tied round the trees, marking them out as hers, and defying the enemy or any one else to touch them. To this day a strip of cocoa-nut leaflets encircling a tree is a sign that it is claimed by some one for a special purpose, and that the nuts there are not to be indiscriminately plucked without permission.

2. Nafanua was also the name of a village god on the island of Upolu. In a case of concealed theft, all the people assembled before the chiefs, and one by one implored vengeance on himself if he was guilty. If all denied, the chiefs wound up the inquiry by shouting

out, "O Nafanua! Compassionate us, let us know who it was, and let speedy death be upon him!"

In war, all assembled to be sprinkled with Nafanua's cocoa-nut water before going to battle. If well done, they conquered; if not, they were driven before the enemy. Confession of offences sometimes preceded the sprinkling, as it was a sign of pardon and purification. Occasional torchlight processions through the village were held in honour of Nafanua. Cases of sickness were also brought and laid before the priest. Those who took fine mats were cured, but shabby offerings of native cloth only prolonged the disease.

17. NAVE.

Nave was the name of a village god on the island of Tutuila. It was represented by a stone called Maa o Nave, or the stone of Nave. This was abbreviated and euphonised into Amanave, and is the name of the village to this day.

18. NONIA.

This was the name of a village god, and was supposed to be incarnate in the cockle. If this shell-fish was eaten by any one of the place a cockle would grow on his nose. If one was picked up and taken away from the shore, a cockle would appear on some part of that person's body.

May was the usual month for feasting and prayers to Nonia, for the removal of coughs and other ailments usually prevalent during that time of transition from the wet to the dry months. On the days of worship the people went about with bundles of cockles, and through them prayed to Nonia.

19. O Le Nifo Loa—*The long tooth.*

This was the name of a disease-making god, said to have come from Fiji and taken up his abode about the south side of Savaii. People, canoes, or property of any kind belonging to that place, were supposed to be media by which the long tooth might be conveyed and cause disease and death. One day the tooth was visible to an old lady, and struck by some scalding greens which she threw at it, and ever after it was crooked and not so deadly. If a person recovered it was said that the tooth must have had the crook running *outside* of the wound, and *vice versa* in a case of death.

To this day the long tooth superstition is a nuisance. A few years ago some people went to that part of Savaii to buy a canoe. They did not get it, but, from a number of deaths soon after at their village, they believed that the tooth had followed them. After a battle ten years ago a man from the long tooth district in Savaii who had been killed, was buried in a village in Upolu. After a time a young chief died there rather suddenly. The tooth was suspected by some of the old people, and so they dug up the bones of the man who had died in battle four years before, and threw them away into the sea, far off outside the reef, so as to rid the land, as they supposed, from the long tooth enemy. Like the celebrated tooth of Buddha at Ceylon, visited by the Prince of Wales in 1875, about which kings fought, the attempt to burn which burst the furnace, and, although buried deep in the earth and trodden down by elephants, managed to come up again, so the long tooth god of Samoa continues to come up every now and then after a sudden death or a prolonged disease of the knee joint, or other deadly ailment.

20. Pava.

This was the name of a war god on the south side of Upolu. It was originally the name of a man who came from the east end of the group. He and his wife went to work as usual in the bush, and left their children in the house. The children kindled a fire to cook some food. Tangaloa, seeing the smoke, came down from the heavens. He found only the children, and inquired where their parents were. Gone to work, said they. "Go and tell them I am here." The children ran off and told them there was a chief in the house. Pava made haste home, found Tangaloa, and prepared a bowl of 'ava (*Piper methisticum*) for him. A little child in creeping about the floor upset the 'ava. Tangaloa flew into a rage, and beat the child to death. He again made it live, however, but Pava got up in anger, went out, plucked a taro leaf (*Arum esculentum*), stepped on to it and went off to Fiji. After a time he came back with a son of the king of Fiji, to the amazement of everybody, and when he died had a place in the Samoan pantheon.

His emblem was a taro leaf, and all his adherents in going to battle were known by taro leaf caps. The slain of that particular village were also known by the round leaf cap. Pava was seen in the rainbow. If it was clear and reflected down on the village, that was a good omen; but if it appeared far inland, the sign was bad, and a veto on any fighting for that day at least.

Another story places the killing of the child in the east end of the group, and says that Pava fled from place to place, and from island to island to get away from the presence of Tangaloa. As soon, however, as he reached a fresh place and thought of remaining there, he saw the terrible eye of Tangaloa looking down on him. Off he went to another village or another island, but still the piercing eye of Tangaloa followed him, until he reached the district to which I have referred, and where the dreaded eye was no longer visible.

21. PILI MA LE MAA—*The lizard and the stone.*

These were the names of twin gods, and worshipped at certain villages in time of war, famine, and pestilence. The month of May was a specially fixed time for prayers, and food offerings. The lizard was the guiding incarnation, and carefully watched in times of war. If in going to battle a lizard was seen darting *across* the road, they returned at once. If it ran ahead, however, they were cheered, and went right on to meet the enemy.

Another plan in searching for an omen was to plait cocoa-nut leaves and cover the middle post of the great house, from the floor to the ridge pole, and there the chiefs sat and watched. If a lizard from the roof came *straight* down on the matting, that was a good sign; but if it came down zigzag, the omen was bad, and fighting suspended. Before going to the fight they met and were sprinkled with cocoa-nut juice by the priest, each at the same time uttering the prayer, "May the road I take flow with blood."

22. STONES.

1. Two unchiselled "smooth stones of the stream" were kept in a temple at one of the villages, and guarded with great care. No stranger or over-curious person was allowed to go near the place, under penalty of a beating from the custodians of these gods. They represented good and not malicious death-causing gods. The one made the yams, bread, fruit, and cocoa-nuts, and the other sent fish to the nets.
2. Another stone was carefully housed in another village as the representative of a rain-making god. When there was over-much rain, the stone was laid by the fire and kept heated till fine weather set in. In a time of drought, the priest and his followers dressed up in fine mats, and went in procession to the stream, dipped the stone and prayed for rain.
3. In a road leading to village plantations a stone stood which was said to have been a petrified coward. He and his brother entered into compact that they would be brave in battle, and implored their god that if either fled that one should be changed into a stone. The

day came, the battle was fought, but one of the brothers turned and fled before the face of the enemy, and so was changed into a stone there and then by the god Fe'e. All the people as they passed inland to work in their plantations kissed, or rather "*smelled*" the stone, and in coming back did the same. Death was supposed to be the consequence of the neglect of this mark of deference to the power of the Fe'e.

4.   At the boundary line between two villages there were two stones, said to have been two young men who quarrelled, fought, and killed each other on that very spot, and whose bodies were immediately changed into stones. If any quarrel took place in either of these two villages there was never any general disturbance. "Go and settle it at the stones" was the standing order; and so all who were inclined to be demonstrative in any affair of honesty or honour went to the stones and fought it out. If either of the duellists was knocked down, that was the final settlement. No one else interfered, and so, by common consent in such matters, these two villages were noted for peace and order.

5.   In a district said to have been early populated by settlers from Fiji, a number of fancy Fijian stones were kept in a temple, and worshipped in time of war. The priest, in consulting them, built them up in the form of a wall, and then watched to see how they fell. If they fell to the westward, it was a sign that the enemy there was to be driven; but if they fell to eastward, that was a warning of defeat, and delay in making an attack was ordered accordingly.

The iconoclast native teachers from Tahiti, in the early stage of the mission, when such stones were given up to them, had them taken off to the beach and broken into fragments, and so stamp out at once the heathenism with which they were associated. Hardly a single relic of the kind can be found at the present day.

23. LE SA—*The sacred one.*

1. The name of a war god in several villages, and incarnate in the lizard. Before going to battle the movements of a lizard in a bundle of spears was watched. If the lizard ran about the points of the spears and the outside of the bundle, it was a good omen; but if it rather worked its way into the centre for concealment, it was a bad sign.

    A piece of matting was also spread over one of the posts of the house, and if a lizard was seen coming down on the matting, the sign was good; but if a bare post was chosen by the creature for its descent from the rafters to the floor, it augured ill. If a lizard crossed the path or ran against any one going to battle, that also was an evil omen.

2. In some places Le Sa was incarnate in an owl, was more of an agricultural god, who sent rain and abundance of food, and was worshipped about the month of April. He was prayed to and propitiated with offerings for the removal of caterpillars from the plantations, as they were thought to be servants under his orders to forage and punish. He was supposed to be fond of the bodies of thieves, and to go at once and devour them if prayed to do so. Bad-tempered parents frightened the children by saying that they would call Le Sa to *drink* them up. In cases of sickness the patient went and weeded some piece of bush land as an offering to Le Sa; and the consequence was often a wonderful cure to the indolent dyspeptic!

3. Le Sa in one place was a household god, and incarnate in the centipede. If any one was bitten by the reptile, or otherwise ailing, an offering of a fine mat and a fan was presented, and the god entreated in some such words as:

    "Lord! if you are angry,
    Tell us the reason
    And send recovery."

24. SILI VAAI—*Far-seeing.*

1. This was the name of a village war god, and seen in a bird. Flight of the bird in the direction of the enemy was a good sign, otherwise the omen was bad.
2. This was also the name of a family god, and seen in a star.

25. SA FULU SA—*Of the sacred feather.*

This was the name of a village war god in Upolu. Incarnate in the kingfisher bird, which, if seen flying *before* the troops, was a good sign. If observed to come flying towards the people as they were preparing to start, the omen signified defeat.

26. SAMA—*Yellow.*

The name of the cannibal god of a village in Savaii. He was incarnate as a man, who had human flesh laid before him when he chose to call for it. This man's power extended to several villages, and his descendants are traced to the present day.

27. SALEVAO—*Sacred one of the bush.*

1. This was a war god in a number of villages, and incarnate in a dog— a white one usually. When he wagged his tail, barked, and dashed ahead in sight of the troops of the enemy, it was a good sign; but to retreat or howl was a bad omen.
2. In some places Salevao was a general village god, as well as a war god. A time was fixed for giving thanks for good crops, and prayers were offered for more. Each family took it in turn to provide food, and they feasted until it had gone the round of the village. The family who had a great display of good things was praised; but the stingy, stinted offerers were cursed. After all had prayed and partaken for

the day, nothing was kept for another meal. Whatever was over was thrown away or buried. At one place in Savaii Salevao had a temple in which a priest constantly resided. The sick were taken there and laid down with offerings of fine mats. The priest went out and stroked the diseased part, and recovery was supposed to follow. At this place Salevao was declared to be a good god in raising a plentiful supply of food, and also noted for his power in keeping away other gods. A story is told of a party of gods from Upolu who were on a journey, but on coming to that place left the public highway along the beach and took a circuitous course far inland, owing to their dread of Salevao. He was generous, however, to travelling parties of mortals. When the chiefs laid down a previously arranged number of cooked pigs and other food to visitors, there was an odd one over and above found among the lot, and this they attributed to the special favour of the god (see 11).

A story of his kindness to Nonu, one of his worshippers, relates that when Nonu was on a visit to the King of Tonga, he and the king had a dispute about the age of the moon. Nonu maintained that it was then to be seen in the morning, the king held that it was not visible in the morning. Nonu said he would stake his life on it; and so it was left for the morning to decide. In the night Salevao appeared to Nonu and said to him: "Nonu, you are wrong; the moon is not now seen in the morning. But, lest you should be killed, I will go and be the moon in the horizon to-morrow morning, and make the king believe you were right after all, and so save your life." In the morning Salevao, as the moon, was seen, and Nonu was saved. Such stories added alike to reverence for the god and to the treasury of the priest.

3. Salevao was the name of a family god also, and incarnate in the eel and the turtle. Any one of the family eating such things was taken

ill; and before death they heard the god saying from within the body: "I am killing this man; he ate my incarnation."

In a case of sickness, a cup of kava was made and poured on the ground outside the house as a drink-offering, and the god called by name to come and accept of it and heal the sick.

In another family the head of the household was the priest. At the evening hour, and other times fixed for worship, all were studiously present, as it was supposed that death would be the penalty if any one was absent.

28. SEPO MALOSI—*Sepo the strong.*

1. Was worshipped in Savaii as a war god, and incarnate in the large bat, or flying-fox. While the bat flew before the warriors all was right; but if it turned round and shut up the way, it was a sign of defeat and a warning to go back.
2. But Sepo in many places was a household god. In an inland village family in Upolu he was called the "Lord of the mountain," and incarnate in the domestic fowl and the pigeon. In another family he was seen in a very small fish which is difficult to catch; and by another family he was supposed to be in the prickly sea-urchin (*Echinus*). The penalty of eating this incarnation was death from a supposed growth of a prickly sea-urchin inside the body.

29. SIULEO—*Tail of the voice, or echo.*

This was the name of a village god in Savaii. Said to have come from Tonga, and able to walk on the sea. He was the fisherman's god. He had a fisherman's hut erected for him on the sea-shore, and was supposed to preside over a certain division of coast.

30. TAAFANUA—*Walk the land.*

This was the name of a war god of one of the islands in the east end of the group. It was incarnate in the Ve'a, or rail *(Rallus Pectoralis).* When the bird screeched and flew before, the people went to battle; but if it turned and flew back, they hesitated.

31. TANGALOA LANGI—*Tangaloa of the heavens.*

The derivation of Tangaloa is uncertain. Loa means long, and tanga, a bag; or, as an adjective, freedom from restriction. The unrestricted, or unconditioned, may therefore fairly be regarded as the name of this Samoan Jupiter. Tangaloa langi tuavalu, Tangaloa of the eighth heaven; Tangaloa faatupu nuu, Tangaloa the creator of lands; Tangaloa asiasi nuu, Tangaloa the visitor of lands; Tangaloa lafoai nuu, Tangaloa the abandoner of lands—these were some of the names by which this god superior was known.

1. At one place he was seen in the moon, and principally worshipped in the month of May. He was also incarnate in the Turi, or snipe. At the stated time of worship no one went from home, and no strangers were allowed to pass through the land. Only men were allowed to partake in the offerings of food; women and children were excluded from any share.
2. At another place his image was a large wooden bowl, said to have come from Fiji. He was also supposed to be present in a hollow stone. A temple was built for him there, and called "The house of the gods." It was carefully shut up all round; thinking that if it was not so, the gods would get out and in too easily, and be all the more destructive. Offerings were presented on war occasions; and he was also presented with gifts, and had prayers offered to him, before going to fish, before planting some fresh section of bush land, and

also in times of sickness or special epidemic. It was firmly believed that if there was no prayer to Tangaloa there could be no blessing. Thunder was a sign that the prayer was heard. Slight tremulous reverberation, however, was a sign rather of rejected prayer and threatened punishment.

3.   In another district Tangaloa was said to have come along the ocean in a canoe, with seven of a crew, and to have taken up his abode in the bush inland of the settlement. Confused noises from the bush there were supposed to be the murmurs of the gods, and a cause of death in the village.

When war broke out two of the chiefs went inland to consult Tangaloa. One sat down in front of the sacred grove of high trees, and the other went round behind. This man was covered from head to foot with leaves, and had only a hole left for the eyes. No creepers ran up the trees, and no leaves were allowed to be seen on the small stones under the trees, as it was supposed the god was in the stones. If the stones appeared separated and unusually far apart, that was a sign that the district was about to be broken up and killed or banished But if the stones were huddled together, that was a good omen, and indicated union, victory, and strength.

32. TAPAAI—*Beckoning*.

This was a war god of a family on Tutuila. He was supposed to be present in a trumpet-shell. When the people were about to go to war the shell was blown by the priest, and all listened. If it blew rough and hollow it was a bad sign; but if clear and euphonic all were cheered, and went off joyfully under the good omen.

33. TAEMA—*Glittering black.*

1. The name of a war god incarnate in the kingfisher bird. If it flew right on before the troops without returning it was a good sign. There was also a temple with only one opening. In times of difficulty the old men of the place went inside and addressed the god, who replied in a human voice, but no body was seen.
2. This was also the name of a goddess said to have been found by some fishermen swimming between Tutuila and Upolu. They covered her with some fine native cloth, and conveyed her to a place in the bush, where they built a temple for her. Offerings of food and fine mats were taken to the place, and laid before two men who acted as priests. On the change from heathenism to Christianity these men had a large quantity of fine mats among the temple treasures. The temple was destroyed, and with the fine mats pigs were bought, and a grand feast was the final adieu to the darkness and follies of the past.
3. In another place Taema was a war god, and present in a bundle of sharks' teeth. These curiosities were done up in a piece of native cloth, and consulted before going to battle. If the bundle felt heavy, that was a bad omen; but if light, the sign was good, and off they went to the fight.
4. Taema and Tila fainga, or Tila the *sportive*, were the goddesses of the tattooers. They swam from Fiji to introduce the craft to Samoa, and on leaving Fiji were commissioned to sing all the way,

    "Tattoo the women, but not the men."

They got muddled over it in the long journey, and arrived at Samoa singing,

    "Tattoo the *men* and not the women."

And hence the universal exercise of the blackening art on the men rather than the women.

5.　Taema and Titi were the names of two household gods in a family at the east end of the group. They were twins, and *Siamese*. Their bodies were united back to back. They swam from the east, and as they came along the one said to the other: "What a pity it is that we can only hear each other's voice, but cannot see each other's face!" On this they were struck by a wave, which cleaved asunder the joining and separated them. Members of the family going on a journey were supposed to have these gods with them as their guardian angels. Everything *double*—such as a double yam, two bananas adhering, etc.—was sacred, and not to be used under penalty of death. It was also forbidden for any member of the family to sit back to back, lest it should be considered mockery and insult to the gods, and incur displeasure.

34. TAISUMALIE—*Tide gently rising.*

1.　This was the name of a lady in Upolu who went away among the gods, was worshipped first by her family, and then by all the people of the land where she resided. She spoke through one of the heads of the family. The bat also was an incarnation, and an unusual number of them came about the temple in time of war. One flying ahead of the troops was always a good omen. If a neighbour killed a bat, it might lead to war to avenge the insult. Another representative of this deity was a shrub (*Ascarina lanceolata*). The leaf of the ti (*Dracaena terminalis*) was carried as a banner wherever the troops went. June was the usual month for special worship. All kinds of food from the land and the sea were provided as a feast, but only the one family of the priest was allowed to partake. Whatever was over after the meal was buried at the beach. After that followed club exercise, and in terrible earnest they battered each other's scalps till the blood streamed down and over their faces and bodies; and this as an offering to the deity. Old and young, men, women, and children, all took part in this general *mêlée* and blood-letting, in the belief that Taisumalie would thereby be all the more pleased with their devotedness, and answer prayer for health, good crops, and success in battle.

2. This was also the name of a war god in Savaii. Incarnate in a man and spoke through him. When the war fleet was about to cross to another island to fight, they went out from the shore half a mile and then returned to a streamlet where they prayed for success, and were sprinkled or purified, and then went off to the fight, free, as they thought, from any delinquency curse which might have been resting upon them.

This deity was also supposed to be incarnate in the sea eel (*Muraena*). In a village where the first Christian native teachers were located one of them caught an eel and had it cooked. Two lads of the place who were their servants ate a bit at the evening meal. As soon as the people heard that these lads had "eaten the god," they mustered, gave them a beating, and dragged them off to a cooking house. They laid them down in the oven pit, and covered them with leaves *as if* they had been killed, and were now to be cooked as a peace-offering to avert the wrath of the deity. It was expected that the lads would immediately die, but as nothing amiss happened to them beyond the weals of the rods used by mortals, it was concluded that Taisumalie was a mere sham, and that they had better now turn to the God of heaven.

3. Taisumalie was also the name of a household god, and worshipped among various families in different parts of the group.

    (1.) In one place a member of the family was the incarnation, and consulted on everything of importance. Before going to war each one would ask whether he should go, what was to befall him, etc. If wounds or death were predicted, the person would perhaps turn round and beat the priest for giving *such* a response!

(2.)   In another place this god was incarnate in an old man who acted as the doctor of the family. The neighbours also took in their sick to him. His principal remedy was to rub the affected part with oil, and then shout out at the top of his voice five times the word Taisumalie, and five times also call him to come and heal. This being done, the patient was dismissed to wait a recovery. On recovery the family had a feast over it, poured out on the ground a cup of kava to the god, thanked for healing and health, and prayed that he might continue to turn his *back* towards them for protection, and set his *face* against all the enemies of the family.

(3.)   To another family he was incarnate in the cuttle-fish (*Octopus*). To another in the mullet. To another in the turtle. If, through a stranger or by any member of the family, an incarnation had been cooked in the family oven, it could not be used again until some one had been laid there as a mock burnt-offering, and gone through the "make-believe" process of cooking. It was death to the family if the oven was used without this ceremony.

35. TILI TILI—*Swift*.

A village god in Upolu, noted for mischief-making, and supposed to be the cause of quarrels, war, and darkness. Seen in the lightning. If there was much of it in a time of war it was believed that the god had come to help and direct. Constant lightning in a particular place indicated an ambushment of the enemy. Continued flashes in front was a sign that the troops of the enemy were driven. But if the lightning moved from the front backwards, that betokened danger, and was an order to retreat.

36. Titi Usi—*Glittering leaf girdle.*

The name of a village god in Savaii, and worshipped at the new moon, when he appeared to them like a bright shining leaf girdle. At that time all work was suspended for a day or two. The cocoa-nut leaf blinds were kept down, and the people sat still in their houses. Any one walking in front of the house risked a beating. After prayer and feasting a man went about and blew a shell-trumpet as a sign to all that the ceremonies were over, and that the usual routine of village and family life might be resumed. Out of respect to the god the name of the leaf girdle, titi, was changed into savalinga, or walking. The said girdle is made of the ti leaves (*Dracaena terminalis*).

37. Tongo—*Mangrove.*

1. This was the name of a war god, and incarnate in the owl. If it hovered over or flew before the troops, that was a sign of victory. If it crossed the path or flew back on them, that was a warning to retreat.

A dead owl found under a tree in the settlement was at once covered over with a piece of white native cloth by the person who discovered it. Then all the village would assemble around it, sit down and beat and bruise their foreheads with any stones they could lay their hands on. This was "an offering of blood" to Tongo, and, with an accompanying death wail, expressed their sympathy with the god over the calamity. Tongo, however, still existed, and was seen in all the remaining owls, which continued to be his incarnations.

2.   There was also a family god of this name, and incarnate in the mullet. If any one of that household ate a piece of that fish it brought on a curse in the form of a *squint*.

38. Tu—*Stand*.

Stand was the name of this war god, as he was said never to sit down. He was incarnate in the rail. If the bird appeared reddish and glossy, it was a sign the people were to go to war. If dark and dingy, the omen was bad, and they were ordered to sit still.

39. Tufi—*To pick up*.

A cocoa-nut tree spear ten feet long was the idol representative of this war god. When the people met for worship the spear was stood up, and offerings were laid before it. It was taken in the war fleet also as a sign that Tu was with them.

In time of peace Tu was a doctor, and supposed to be powerful in removing sickness in return for prayers and offerings.

40. Turia—*Driven*.

This was the name of a god in Savaii by whose help a district once fought and conquered against fearful odds. He was of use in peace also as well as in times of war. He could change the drought into rainy weather, and this again into sunshine. He was also supposed to come with his share of food for the entertainment of strangers, and add a pig to the number prepared by the people. If six were laid down, the guests found, when they separated the heap of dainties they had received, that there would be *seven* instead of six. The trick of adding secretly a pig was carried on by some of the priesthood, and, in the eyes of the credulous multitude, added vastly to the wonder-working power of Turia. On another island the shrine of Turia was a very smooth stone in a sacred grove. The priest was careful to weed all round about, and covered it with branches to keep the god warm. When praying on account of war, drought, famine, or epidemic, the branch *clothes* were carefully renewed. No one dared to touch this stone, lest a poisonous and deadly influence of some kind should at once radiate from it to the transgressor.

41. TUIFITI—*King of Fiji.*

This was the name of a village god in Savaii supposed to be incarnate in a man who walked about but was never visible to the people of the place. He could be seen, however, by strangers. For instance, if a large travelling party were spending a day at the settlement, and entertained in the usual way by every inhabitant turning out to march in procession to the guests, each with a basket of cooked food, the god would be among them. This was known by two things. First, more pigs by one, two, or three than the chiefs arranged to provide; and secondly, by the guests after the ceremony putting such a question as, "Whose son was that handsome young man dressed with a girdle of fancy bush leaves?" while at the same time no one of the place had seen such a person.

The special abode of Tuifiti was a grove of large and durable trees called Ifilele, or *Afzelia bijuga.* No one dared to cut that timber. A story is told of a party from Upolu who once attempted it, and the consequence was that *blood* flowed from the tree and that the sacrilegious strangers all took ill and died. In later times the trees fell harmlessly under the axes of the villagers, and were very useful in building a house for their missionary.

42. TUNA MA FATA—*The Eel and the Litter.*

There are two mountains at the west end of Upolu with a stream between them. On the one mountain Tuna lived, and on the other Fata.

They were in the habit of meeting at the stream close by the habitat of a great eel. With this they amused themselves by taking it out of the water and carrying it about shoulder high on a litter.

43. Vave—*Swift*.

1.   This was the name of a war god in Savaii, said to have come from Tonga, and incarnate in the Manualii (*Porphyris Samoensis*). Bird of Lii, or Bird of Chiefs, the word may be translated. If it flew about and behind the war party, they were encouraged and sure of victory; but if the bird fluttered about before them, it was a sign of defeat. Again, if in time of peace it was seen pecking at the ridge pole of the house, that was a sign of a coming disturbance, and the pressure of some heavy fine. When the people mustered in the village for battle, and before going off to meet the enemy, they were first of all sprinkled with the juice of a cocoa-nut, and then all united with the priest in the following prayer:—

>   "Our own Lord Vave!
>   Level up the stumps of the trees,
>   Take away the rough stones,
>   Give light to our eyes,
>   And let blood flow in our path."

2.   In another village in Upolu Vave was incarnate in a pigeon which was carefully kept and fed by the different members of the family in turn. But the special residence of Vave there was an old tree inland of the village which was a "place of refuge" for murderers and other capital offenders. If that tree was reached by the criminal he was safe, and the avenger of blood could pursue no farther, but wait investigation and trial. It is said that the king of a division of Upolu, called Atua, once lived at that spot. After he died the house fell into

decay, but the tree was fixed on as representing the departed king, and out of respect for his memory it was made the substitute of a living and royal protector. It was called "O le asi pulu tangata," *the asi tree the refuge of men*. This reminds me of what I once heard from a native of another island. He said that at one time they had been ten years without a king, and so anxious were they to have some protecting substitute, that they fixed upon a large O'a tree (*Bischoffia Javanica*), and made it the representative of a king, and an asylum for the thief or the homicide when pursued by the injured in hot haste for vengence.

3. Vave was also the name of a war god in another village, and incarnate in the Ve'a, or rail bird. When it was heard chattering, or "scolding," as they called it, at midnight, it prognosticated an attack next day, and they would at once send off the women and children to a place of safety. When offerings of food were presented at the temple of Vave, long poles were erected, one at each corner, and these were covered with fragrant-scented leaves and flowers. When they started to fight they prayed and professed to be guided by the flight of the Ve'a. If it flew before them that was enough, they followed. A notable instance of the power of Vave is given in an account of the battle with the Tongan invaders. Many were killed in single combat by a hero called One. Vave was once more implored to help, and that very day One was killed at a single blow by a chief called Tuato, and hence the proverb which obtains to the present day:

> "Ua 'ai tasi Tuato, or
> Tuato bites but once."

The power of Vave was again seen in another way. A number of gods came to raise a rocky precipice right between the village and the ocean. Vave, however, was immediately up in arms against them, and drove them off for miles along the coast into another district, where they effected their object and made the beach there a great high iron-bound shore, which remains to the present day.

4.   In another place Vave was the name of a household god, and incarnate in the eel. If any one of the family was sick, Vave was prayed to in the evening. Next morning a search was made among the bundles of mats and other property. If an eel was found among them it was a sign of death; if not, it was a sign of recovery.

CHAPTER V.

GODS INFERIOR, OR HOUSEHOLD GODS.

1. ALOIMASINA—*Child of the Moon.*

This was the name of a household god, and seen in the moon. On the appearance of the new moon all the members of the family called out: "Child of the moon, you have come." They assembled also, presented offerings of food, had a united feast, and joined in the prayer:

> "Oh, child of the moon!
> Keep far away
> Disease and death."

They also prayed thus before leaving the house to go to battle:

> "Oh, child of the moon!
> Bury up your hollows
> And stumps of trees
> And lumpy stones
> For our running at ease."

2. APELESA—*Sacred fulness.*

1. In one family this god was incarnate in the turtle. While one of the family dared not partake, he would help a neighbour to cut up and cook one; only while he was doing that, he had a bandage tied over his mouth lest some embryo turtle should slip down his throat, grow up, and cause his death.
2. In another family Apelesa spoke at times through an old man. When an oven of food was opened the first basket was hung up on the outside of one of the posts of the house for the god. If the rats, or a dog, or any hungry mortal took it in the night, it was supposed that Apelesa chose to come in *that* form for his offering. He was also considered the guardian of the family, and if any other gods came about he frightened them away.
3. In another family a woman called Alaiava, or *means of entertainment*, was priestess of Apelesa. She prayed at parturition times, and in cases of severe illness. Her usual mode of acting the doctor was, first of all, to order down all the cocoa-nut leaf window-blinds of one end of the house. She then went into the darkened place. Presently that end of the house shook as if by an earthquake, and when she came out she declared what the disease was, and ordered corresponding treatment; the result was that, "some recovered, and some died."

In this family the first basket of cooked food was also sacred to the god, but their custom was to take it and hang it up in the large house of the village where passing travellers were accustomed to call and rest. No one of the village dared to touch that basket without risking the wrath of the god. Any passing *stranger*, however, was as welcome to partake as if he had been specially sent for it by Apelesa.

3. Asomua—*First Day.*

This was a household god, and particularly useful to the family in detecting and telling out the name of the thief when anything was missed. He was called *first day*, as it was supposed that he existed in the world before mortals.

4. Leatualoa—*The long god, or the centipede.*

This was the name of a god seen in the centipede. A tree near the house was the residence of the creature. When any one of the family was ill, he went out with a fine mat and spread it under the tree, and there waited for the centipede to come down. If it came down and crawled *under* the mat, that was a sign that the sick person was to be covered over with mats and buried. If, however, it crawled on the top of the mat, that was a sign of recovery.

5. O Le Aumâ—*The red liver.*

This family god was seen, or incarnate, in the wild pigeon. If any visitor happened to roast a pigeon while staying there, some member of the household would pay the penalty by being done up in leaves, as if ready to be baked, and carried and laid in the *cool* oven for a time, as an offering to show their unabated regard to Aumâ.

The use of the reddish-seared bread-fruit leaf for any purpose was also insulting to this deity. Such leaves were in common use as *plates* on which to hand a bit of food from one to another, but that particular family dared not use them under a penalty of being seized with rheumatic swellings, or an eruption all over the body called tangosusu, and resembling chicken-pox.

6. Iulautalo—*Ends of the taro leaf.*

To this family god the *ends* of leaves and other things were considered sacred, and not to be handled or used in any way. In daily life it was no small trouble to this particular household to cut off the ends of all the taro, bread-fruit, and cocoa-nut leaves which they required for culinary purposes. Ends of taro, yams, bananas, fish, etc., were also carefully laid aside, and considered as unfit to be eaten as if they were poison. In a case of sickness, however, the god allowed, and indeed required, that the patient should be fanned with the *ends* of cocoa-nut leaflets.

7. O Le Alii O Fiti—*The Chief of Fiji.*

This was the name of a god in a certain household, and present in the form of an eel, and hence the eel was never used by them as an article of food. This god was supposed to be unusually kind, and never injured any of the family. They showed their gratitude by presenting the first fruits of their taro plantation.

8. Limulimuta—*Sea-weed.*

This was the name by which another protector was known. If any members of the family went to fight at sea, they collected some sea-weed to take with them. If in pursuit of a canoe, they threw out some of it to hinder the progress of the enemy, and make the chase successful in obtaining a decapitated head or two. If the enemy tried to pick up any of this deified sea-weed it immediately sank, but rose again and floated on the surface if one of its friends paddled up to the spot.

9. Moso'oi.

This is the name of a tree (*Conanga Odorata*), the yellow flowers of which are highly fragrant. In one place it was supposed to be the habitat of a household god, and anything aromatic or sweet-scented which the family happened to get was presented as an offering.

At any household gathering the god was sent for to be present. Three different messengers had to go at short intervals, as it was not expected that he would come before the *third* appeal or entreaty for his presence.

10. FATUPUAA MA LE FEE—*The pig's heart and the octopus.*

Another family supposed that two of their gods were embodied in the said heart and octopus. Men, women, and children of them were most scrupulous never to eat either the one or the other, believing that such a meal would be the swallowing of a germ of a living heart or octopus growth, by which the insulted gods would bring about death.

11. PU'A.

This is the name of a large tree (*Hernandia Peltata*). A family god of the same name was supposed to live in it, and hence no one dared to pluck a leaf or break a branch.

The same god was also supposed to be incarnate in the octopus, and also in the land crab. If one of these crabs found its way into the house, it was a sign that the head of the house was about to die.

12. SAMANI.

This was the name of a family god. It was seen in the turtle, the sea eel, the octopus, and the garden lizard. Any one eating or injuring such things had either to be *sham* baked in an unheated oven, or drink a quantity of rancid oil as penance and a purgative. This god predicted that there was a time coming when Samoa would be filled with foreign gods.

13. SATIA.

1. In one place the member of the family supposed to be the priest of the god was noted for cannibalism. At times he would cry out furiously and order those about him to be off and get him some of his "sacred food." He professed to be doctor as well as demon. A great chief when ill was once taken to him, and the doctor's bill for a cure was the erection of a mound of stones, on the top of which a house was to be built. The bill was paid by the retinue of the chief.
2. In another family it was supposed that their god Satia had the power to become incarnate in a man or a woman. If he wished to go to a particular woman, he became a man; and if he desired a man, he changed into a woman.

14. SENGI VAVE—*Snatch quickly.*

An old man named Sengi, or *snatch*, was an incarnation of this household god. All the fine mats and other valuables were in some mysterious way under his control. On returning from any kind of daily work in the bush every one on entering the house had to salute him, as the representative of the god, in some apologetic phrase, such as "I beg your pardon." If any one omitted this mark of respect, the penalty was the disappearance of a fine mat from the family bundle without any one knowing how it was taken.

15. SOESAI.

This was the name of a household god in some families. In one, the god was seen in the domestic fowl. In another, the incarnations were the eel, the octopus, and turtle. Prayers for life and recovery were offered in cases of great danger, and also at child-birth.

16. Si'u—*Extremity or end.*

The family in which this god was worshipped said that he appeared in the form of a *skull* once a year, about the month of May. Lemana, or the Powerful, was the name of the priest. If in time of famine or pestilence the family had been preserved thanks were specially offered to Lemana for having been so successful in his pleadings with the god.

17. Sina 'Ai Mata—*Sina the eye-eater.*

This god was incarnate in the bird called Ve'a, and was the juvenile scarecrow of the family. "Do not make such a noise; Sina, the eye-eater, will come and pick out your eyes." The eyes of fish were sacred to this god, and never eaten by any of the family.

18. Tongo.

1. In one family this god was incarnate in the bat, and was supposed to be specially attentive to turmeric. When a party of women were met to grate the root and prepare some of this native dye and cosmetic they usually had some food together. If at such a time a woman concealed a tit-bit to eat by the sly, when she came to put it to her mouth it had been changed into *turmeric* by the anger and power of Tongo.
2. The stinging ray fish was the incarnation of Tongo in another family. If they heard of any neighbour who had caught a fish of the sort, they would go and beg them to give it up and not to cook it. A refusal would be followed by a fight.
3. In another family Tongo was incarnate in the mullet, and the penalty for eating that fish by any of them was a disease ending in a squint.

19. Tuialii—*King of Chiefs.*

1. In one family this god was greatly praised as being a good and kind deity. In a time of scarcity, for instance, he led them to some place in the bush where they could dig up plenty of wild yams.
2. In another family this god was prayed to for life and health before the evening meal; an offering of a blazing fire was essential to the success of the prayer, which ran as follows:—

"This is our fire to you, it burns bright; other fires are dim and going out; send these families to the lower regions, but give us life and health."

The sea eel, octopus, and mullet were incarnations of this god. He was also seen in the *ends* of banana leaves. If any one used the end of a banana leaf as a cap, baldness was the punishment. All the children born in the family were called by the name of the god.

20. Tuipangota—*The King of Criminals.*

A household god, and the special guardian of a particular family against thieving. If any thing was stolen the unknown culprit was given over by prayer to be put to death in some way by Tuipangota. A raised stone platform was erected in the house on which he was supposed to sit, and close beside it was another to serve the purpose of an altar, on which offerings were laid.

21. Taumanupepe—*Fight creature butterfly.*

This family god was incarnate in butterflies. Any one of that household catching or killing these beautiful winged insects were liable to be struck dead by the god.

In another family this god was supposed to have three mouths. There it was forbidden to drink from a cocoa-nut shell water-bottle which had all the three eyes or openings perforated. Only one, or at the most two, apertures for drinking were allowed. A third would be a mockery, and bring down the wrath of his butterflyship.

22. ULAVAI—*Fresh-water prawn, or crayfishes.*

This was a household god in a family in one of the villages of Aana. A woman had been bathing and brought on a premature event which happens sometimes. When she told her friends they went to search for the child. Nothing could be seen, however, but an unusual number of prawns or crayfishes, into which they supposed the infant had been changed. And so they commenced to regard the crayfish as the incarnation of a new household god, gave it food, and offered prayers before it for family prosperity.

To these may be added the names of forty-six other gods, making in all one hundred and ten, but of whom I have little to say different from the descriptions of Samoa Zoolatry, etc., already given. A few more are referred to in the Cosmogony and other details, making up the number of Samoan deities of which I have heard to about a hundred and twenty, all claiming and receiving the two essentials of religion—something to be believed and something to be done.

CHAPTER VI.

THE PEOPLE—INFANCY AND CHILDHOOD.

At the birth of her child, the mother had a liberal share in the kind attentions of her friends. Her own mother was almost invariably *la sage-femme*; but, failing her, some other female friend. Her father was generally present on the occasion, and either he or her husband prayed to the household god, and promised to give any offering he might require, if he would only preserve mother and child in safety. A prayer was thus expressed: "O Moso, be propitious; let this my daughter be preserved alive! Be compassionate to us; save my daughter, and we will do anything you wish as our redemption price." Offerings to the god, as we have already seen, were regulated by the caprice and covetousness of the cunning priest. Sometimes a canoe was demanded; at other times a house was to be built; and often fine mats or other valuable property was required. The household god of the family of the father was generally prayed to first; but, if the case was tedious or difficult, the god of the family of the mother was then invoked; and when the child was born, the mother would call out: "Who were you praying to?" and the god prayed to just before was carefully remembered and its incarnation duly acknowledged throughout the future life of the child. By way of respect to him the child was called his *merda*; and was actually named during infancy and childhood "merda of Tongo," or "Satiâ," or whatever other deity it might be. If the little stranger was a boy, the umbilical cord was cut on a club, that he might grow up to be brave in war. If of the other sex, it was done on the board on which they beat out the bark of which they make their native cloth. Cloth-making is the work of women; and their wish was that the little girl should grow up and prove useful to the family in her proper occupation.

Infanticide, as it prevailed in Eastern Polynesia and elsewhere, was unknown in Samoa. Nor were children ever exposed. After they were born they were affectionately cared for. But the custom of destroying them *before* that prevailed to a melancholy extent. Shame, fear of punishment, lazy unwillingness to nurse, and a dread of soon being old-looking, were the prevailing causes. Pressure was the means employed, and in some cases proved the death of the unnatural parent.

As to nursing, during the first two or three days the nurse bestowed great attention to the head of the child, that it might be modified and shaped after notions of propriety and beauty. The child was laid on its back, and the head surrounded with three flat stones. One was placed close to the crown of the head, and one on either side. The forehead was then pressed with the hand, that it might be flattened. The nose, too, was carefully flattened. Our "canoe noses," as they call them, are blemishes in their estimation. For the first three days the infant was fed with the juice of the chewed kernel of the cocoa-nut, pressed through a piece of native cloth, and dropped into the mouth. On the third day a woman of the sacred craft was sent for to examine the milk. A little was put into a cup, with water and two heated stones, and then examined. If it had the slightest curdled appearance she pronounced it bitter and poisonous. This process she repeated two or three times a day for several days, until it was drawn off free from coagulation, and then she pronounced it sweet and wholesome, and the child was forthwith permitted to partake of its proper nourishment. Of course she was well paid for her services, and had every inducement to prolong them for several days. During this time the infant was fed with the juice of the cocoa-nut or the sugar-cane. Many fell victims to this improper treatment. At a very early period the child was fed, and sometimes weaned altogether at four months. This was another fruitful source of mortality among children. Occasionally the father, or some member of the family, through whom it was supposed the god of the family spoke, expressly ordered that the child have nothing but the breast for an indefinite time. This was a mark of respect to the god, and called his "banana." In these cases the child grew amazingly, and was soon, literally, as plump as a banana.

A modified form of *circumcision* prevailed. About the eighth or tenth year two or three boys would unite and go of their own accord to some one in the village, who would make the customary incision, and give him some trifling reward for his trouble. There was no further ceremony on the occasion, as at other periods of life.

Names.—Out of respect to the household god, as we have already remarked, the child was named after him, during the time of infancy and childhood; after that, a name was given. The animal and vegetable kingdoms, places, occupations, actions, and passing events, furnished them with the principal names. The primitive rule, "one man, one word," invariably prevailed. Occasionally a chief bore the name of one of the gods superior.

Rejoicing.—About the third day the woman was up and at her usual occupation, and ready to take part in the rejoicings connected with the occasion. By this time the principal friends were assembled. They all brought presents, and observed an unvarying rule in the *kind* of presents each was expected to bring. The relations of the husband brought "*oloa*," which included pigs, canoes, and all kinds of foreign property. The relations of the wife brought "*tonga*," which included the leading articles manufactured by the females—viz. fine mats and native cloth. The "*oloa*" brought by the friends of the husband was all distributed among those of the wife, and the "*tonga*" brought by the friends of the wife was divided among those of the husband; and thus the whole affair was so managed that the friends were the benefited parties chiefly, and the husband and wife left no richer than they were. Still, they had the satisfaction of having seen what they considered a great honour—viz. heaps of property collected on occasion of the birth of their child. Feasting, sham-fighting, night-dancing, and many other heathen customs, formed one continued scene of revelry for two or three days, when the party broke up. When the child became strong and able to sit there was another feast for "the sitting of the child." A third feast was for the "creeping of the child." A fourth when the child was able to stand, and called "the standing feast." But the greatest was the *fifth*, when the child could walk. Then there was singing and night-dances, and then, too, if the child danced and sang, and was "impudent," the parents boasted over its abilities.

Twins were rare. Triplets still more so; indeed, there is only a vague tradition of such a thing. Twins were supposed to be of one mind, and to think, feel, and act alike, during the time of infancy and childhood at least. There were a few instances of large families, but four or five would be the average.

Adopted Children.—The number of children seen in a family was small, occasioned, to a great extent, by the bad management and consequent mortality of children, and also a custom which prevailed of parting with their children to friends who wished to adopt them. The general rule was for the husband to give away his child to his sister. She and her husband gave, in return for the child, some foreign property, just as if they had received so many fine mats or native cloth. The adopted child was viewed as "*tonga*" and was, to the family who adopted it, a channel through which native property (or "*tonga*") continued to flow to that family from the parents of the child. On the other hand, the child was to its parents a source of obtaining foreign property (or "*oloa*") from the parties who adopted it, not only at the time of its adoption, but as long as the child lived. Hence the custom of adoption was not so much the want of natural affection as the sacrifice of it to this systematic facility of traffic in native and foreign property. Hence, also, parents may have had in their family adopted children, and their own real children elsewhere.

70

Employments.—Girls always, and boys for four or five years, were under the special charge of the mother, and followed her in domestic avocations. The girl was taught to draw water, gather shell-fish, make mats and native cloth. The boy after a time followed his father, and soon became useful in planting, fishing, house-building, and all kinds of manual labour. Boys were also accustomed to club together, and wander about the settlement, the plantation, or in the bush. If they fell in with a fallen cocoa-nut one boy would sit down and name some to come and join him in eating it, and to the rest he would call out, "Go and catch butterflies." Hence one who is excluded from eating anything nice is called *a butterfly-catcher*. If they called at the residence of one of themselves, then perhaps the lad of that house would select some to have food with him there, and call them "cocoa-nut princes," and the rest he would send off, calling them "cocoanut pigs." The latter would go off offended, and vow to each other never again to be friendly with that stingy, *stunted* fellow! The following is a translated specimen of one of the old songs chanted for the diversion of children, or to lessen the tedium of a long canoe journey. I do not tamper with an exact translation by any attempt at rhythm or rhyme, but simply give the thoughts as they stand, and as a fair translation would explain them.:—

1. Mailesaeia and Mailetupengia were married.
They had two children, and these were their names,
The boy Tulifauiave, and the girl Sinataevaeva.
 Chorus—Aue! or *wonderful!*

2. They were unkind to their children, and deserted them;
They did not wish to have children.
 etc.

3. Then said the girl to the boy: "Come let us go,
Let us seek another home," and away they wandered.

        etc.

4. They called at the house of Tangaloa of the heavens,
And Tangaloa took the girl and married her.

        etc.

5. The brother of the girl acted as their child.
He was a lovely boy, and grew up to be a beauty.

        etc.

6. Tangaloa of the heavens became jealous of the lad,
And told his people to kill him.

        etc.

7. They took him to the bush and killed him,
He yielded to their wishes and resisted not.

        etc.

8. They were divided about the disposal of the body,
Some said throw it into the river, others said leave it in the bush.

        etc.

9. They cast it into the river to float to the sea,
It came floating down, and there his sister stood on the beach.

        etc.

10. She screamed, and wept, and wailed;
She seized the body, patted his head, and prayed for life.

        etc.

11. The wounds closed up and healed, the lad sat up,
And thus he spake: "Let us both be off together."

etc.

12. They went to the village, the people were in the bush;
They smashed every canoe but one, and in that they left,
To search for the land of their parents.

etc.

13. The people returned from work, no Sinataevaeva was there,
Tangaloa called for his daughters Darkness, Lightning, and Thunder,
And ordered them off in search of his wife.

etc.

14. The three daughters obeyed, Thunder roared and Lightning flashed,
Darkness and Storm were added, and the canoe was found.

etc.

15. The ladies shouted out: "Don't be afraid; all's well!
You two be off, a calm and a smooth sea to you!
'Twas cruel to kill a child yonder."

etc.

16. The two went on and reached their land and home,
First the boy went on shore, his sister remained in the canoe.

etc.

17. Their parents called out: "Where are you two going?"
"My sister and I are in search of the home of our parents."

etc.

18. "Who are your parents, tell us their names?"
"Mailesaeia and Mailetupengia," replied the lad.

etc.

19. Out rushed the parents in tears,
The children they cast away had come back,
And now their love returned to them.

etc.

CHAPTER VII.

ADULT AND ADVANCED YEARS.

Passing from infancy and childhood we proceed to the ceremonies, superstitions, and customs connected with more advanced years.

Tattooing.—"Herodotus found among the Thracians that the barbarians could be exceedingly foppish after their fashion. The man who was not tattooed among them was not respected." It was the same in Samoa. Until a young man was tattooed, he was considered in his minority. He could not think of marriage, and he was constantly exposed to taunts and ridicule, as being poor and of low birth, and as having no right to speak in the society of men. But as soon as he was tattooed he passed into his majority, and considered himself entitled to the respect and privileges of mature years. When a youth, therefore, reached the age of sixteen, he and his friends were all anxiety that he should be tattooed. He was then on the outlook for the tattooing of some young chief with whom he might unite. On these occasions, six or a dozen young men would be tattooed at one time; and for these there might be four or five tattooers employed.

Tattooing is still kept up to some extent, and is a regular profession, just as house-building, and well paid. The custom is traced to Taçmâ and Tilafainga (see p. 55); and they were worshipped by the tattooers as the presiding deities of their craft.

The instrument used in the operation is an oblong piece of human bone (*os ilium*), about an inch and a half broad and two inches long. A time of war and slaughter was a harvest for the tattooers to get a supply of instruments. The one end is cut like a small-toothed comb, and the other is fastened to a piece of cane, and looks like a little serrated adze. They dip it into a mixture of candle-nut ashes and water, and, tapping it with a little mallet, it sinks into the skin; and in this way they puncture the whole surface over which the tattooing extends. The greater part of the body from the waist down to the knee is covered with it, variegated here and there with neat regular stripes of the untattooed skin, which when they are well oiled, make them appear in the distance as if they had on black silk knee-breeches. Behrens, in describing these natives in his narrative of Roggewein's voyage of 1772, says: "They were clothed from the waist downwards with fringes and a kind of silken stuff artificially wrought." A nearer inspection would have shown that the "fringes" were a bunch of red *ti* leaves (*Dracæna terminalis*) glistening with cocoa-nut oil, and the "kind of silken stuff," the tattooing just described. As it extends over such a large surface the operation is a tedious and painful affair. After smarting and bleeding for a while under the hands of the tattooers, the patience of the youth is exhausted. They then let him rest and heal for a time, and, before returning to him again, do a little piece on each of the party. In two or three months the whole is completed. The friends of the young men are all the while in attendance with food. They also bring quantities of fine mats and native cloth, as the hire of the tattooers; connected with them, too, are many waiting on for a share in the food and property.

The waste of time, revelling, and immorality connected with the custom have led many to discountenance it; and it is, to a considerable extent, given up. But the gay youth still thinks it manly and respectable to be tattooed; parental pride says the same thing; and so the custom still obtains. It is not likely, however, to stand long before advancing civilisation. European clothing, and a sense of propriety they are daily acquiring, lead them to cover the tattooed part of the body entirely; and, when its display is considered a shame rather than a boast, it will probably be given up as painful, expensive, and useless; and then, too, instead of the tattooing, age, experience, common-sense, and education will determine whether or not the young man is entitled to the respect and privileges of mature years.

There was a custom observed by the other sex worth noticing, for the sake of comparison with other parts of the world. About the time of entering into womanhood, their parents and other relatives collected a quantity of fine mats and cloth, prepared a feast, and invited all the unmarried women of the settlement. After the feast the property was distributed among them, and they dispersed. None but females were present. It was considered mean and a mark of poverty if a family did not thus observe the occasion.

Chastity was ostensibly cultivated by both sexes; but it was more a name than a reality. From their childhood their ears were familiar with the most obscene conversation; and as a whole family, to some extent, herded together, immorality was the natural and prevalent consequence. There were exceptions, especially among the daughters of persons of rank; but they were the exceptions, not the rule.

Adultery, too, was sadly prevalent, although often severely punished by private revenge. If the injured husband sought revenge in the blood of the seducer no one thought he had done wrong. But the worst feature of the law of private revenge was that the brother, or any near relation of the culprit, was as liable to be killed as himself.

Marriage contracts were never entered into before the parties reached the years of maturity just described. Considerable care was taken to prevent any union between near relatives; so much so, that a list of what they deemed improper marriages would almost compare with the "Table of kindred and affinity." They say that, of old, custom and the gods frowned upon the union of those in whom consanguinity could be closely traced. Few had the hardihood to run in the face of superstition; but if they did, and their children died at a premature age, it was sure to be traced to the anger of the household god on account of the forbidden marriage.

A young man rarely, in the first instance, paid his addresses in person to the object of his choice. A present of food was taken to her and her relatives by a friend of his, who was, at the same time, commissioned to convey the proposal to her father; or, failing him, to the elder brother of the young woman. Her consent was, of course, asked too; but that was a secondary consideration. She had to agree if her parents were in favour of the match. If the present of food was received and the reply favourable, the matter was considered settled. There was also a somewhat formal meal directly after the marriage ceremony.

All parties consenting, preparations commenced, and one, two, or three months were spent collecting various kinds of property. All the family and relatives of the bride were called upon to assist, and thus they raised a great quantity of *tonga*, which included all kinds of fine mats and native cloth, manufactured by the women. This was invariably the dowry presented to the bridegroom and his friends on the celebration of the nuptials. He and his friends, on the other hand, collected in a similar manner for the family of the bride *oloa*, which included canoes, pigs, and foreign property of any kind which might fall into their hands, such as knives, hatchets, trinkets, cloth, garments, etc., received through a Tongan canoe or a passing vessel.

A time was fixed when the parties assembled. The bride and her friends, taking with them her dowry, proceeded to the home of the bridegroom, which might be in another settlement, or on an adjacent island. If they were people of rank it was the custom that the ceremonies of the occasion pass off in the marae. The marae is the forum or place of public assembly—an open circular space, surrounded by bread-fruit trees, under the shade of which the people sit. Here the bridegroom and his friends and the whole village assembled, together with the friends of the bride. All were seated cross-legged around the marae, glistening from head to foot with scented oil, and decked off with beads, garlands of sweet-smelling flowers, and whatever else their varying fancy might suggest for the joyous occasion. In a house close by the bride was seated. A pathway from this house to the marae, in front of where the bridegroom sits, was carpeted with fancy native cloth; and, all being ready, the bride, decked off with beads, a garland of flowers or fancy shells, and girt round the waist with fine mats, flowing in a train five or six feet behind her, moved slowly along towards the marae. She was followed along the carpeted pathway by a train of young women, dressed like herself, each bearing a valuable mat, half spread out, holding it to the gaze of the assembly; and, when they reached the bridegroom, the mats were laid down before him. They then returned to the house for more, and went on renewing the procession and display until some fifty or a hundred fine mats and two or three hundred pieces of native cloth were heaped before the bridegroom. This was the dowry. The bride then advanced to the bridegroom and sat down. By-and-by she rose up before the assembly, and was received with shouts of applause, and, as a further expression of respect, her immediate friends, young and old, took up stones and beat themselves until their heads were bruised and bleeding. The obscenity to prove her virginity which preceded this burst of feeling will not bear the light of description. Then followed a display of the *oloa* (or property) which the bridegroom presented to the friends of the bride. Then they had dinner, and after that, the distribution of the property. The father, or, failing him, the brother or sister of the father of the bridegroom, had the disposal of the *tonga* which formed the dowry; and on the other hand, the father or brother of the bride had the disposal of the property which was given by the bridegroom. Night-dances and their attendant immoralities wound up the ceremonies.

The marriage ceremonies of common people passed off in a house, and with less display; but the same obscene form was gone through to which we have referred—a custom which, doubtless, had some influence in cultivating chastity, especially among young women of rank. There was a fear of disgracing themselves and their friends, and a dread of a severe beating from the latter after the ceremony to which the faithless bride was sometimes subjected, almost as if the letter of the Mosaic law had been carried out upon her.

But there were many marriages without any such ceremonies at all. If there was a probability that the parents would not consent, from disparity of rank or other causes, an elopement took place; and, if the young man was a chief of any importance, a number of his associates mustered in the evening, and walked through the settlement, singing his praises and shouting out the name of the person with whom he had eloped. This was sometimes the first intimation the parents had of it, and, however mortified they might be, it was too late. After a time, if the couple continued to live together, their friends acknowledged the union by festivities and an exchange of property.

Concubinage.—When the newly-married woman took up her abode in the family of her husband she was attended by a daughter of her brother, who was, in fact, a concubine. Her brother considered that if he did not give up his daughter for this purpose, he should fail in duty and respect towards his sister, and incur the displeasure of their household god. Failing her brother, her mother's relatives supplied her with this maid of honour. Hence, with his wife, a chief had one, two, or three concubines. Each of these took with her *tonga* as a dowry, which, perhaps, was the most important part of the business, for, after presenting her dowry, she might live with him or not, as she pleased. Often the addition of these concubines to the family was attended with all the display and ceremonies of a regular marriage.

Polygamy.—The marriage ceremony being such a prolific source of festivities and profit to the chief and his friends, the latter, whether he was disposed to do it or not, often urged on another and another repetition of what we have described. They took the thing almost entirely into their own hands, looked out for a match in a rich family, and, if that family was agreeable to it, the affair was pushed on, whether or not the daughter was disposed to it. She, too, as a matter of etiquette, must be attended by her complement of one or more young women. According to this system, a chief might have some ten or a dozen wives and concubines in a short time. Owing, however, to quarrelling and jealousies, many of them soon returned to their parental home; and it was rare to find a chief with more than two wives living with him at the same time.

Divorce.—If the marriage had been contracted merely for the sake of the property and festivities of the occasion, the wife was not likely to be more than a few days or weeks with her husband. With or without leave, she soon found her way home to her parents. If, however, a couple had lived together for years and wished to separate, if they were mutually agreed, they did it in a more formal way. They talked over the matter coolly, made a fair division of their property, and then the wife was conveyed back to her friends, taking with her any young children, and leaving those more advanced with their father. A woman might thus go home and separate entirely from her husband; but, while that husband lived, she dared not marry another. Nor could she marry even after his death, if he was a chief of high rank, without the special permission of the family with which she had connected herself by marriage. Any one who broke through the custom, and married her without this, was liable to have his life taken from him by that family, or at least he had to pay them a heavy fine.

Widows.—The brother of a deceased husband considered himself entitled to have his brother's wife, and to be regarded by the orphan children as their father. If he was already married, she would, nevertheless, live with him as a second wife. In the event of there being several brothers, they met and arranged which of them was to act the part of the deceased brother. The principal reason they alleged for the custom was a desire to prevent the woman and her children returning to her friends, and thereby diminishing the number and influence of their own family. And hence, failing a brother, some other relative would offer himself, and be received by the widow. Should none of them, however, wish to live with her, or should there be any unwillingness on her part, she was, in either case, at liberty to return to her own friends.

The following is a specimen of one of their love songs:—

1. There was Tafitofau and Ongafau, and they had two daughters;
The one was Sinaleuuna and the other Sinaeteva.
The two girls sat and wished they had a brother.
Chorus—Aue!

2. Again Ongafau had a child, and it was a boy.
The child grew up, but his sisters never saw him,
They lived apart from their parents and the boy.
etc.

3. Then Tafitofau and Ongafau said to the boy, who was called Maluafiti ("Shade of Fiji"): "Go with some food to the ladies."
The lad went down, the girls looked and were struck with his beauty,
etc.

4. He came with the food and said he was their brother;
The sisters rejoiced and gave thanks that their desire was granted,
They had now a brother.
etc.

5. Then the sisters sat down and filled into a bamboo bottle
The liquid shadow of their brother.
etc.

6. A report came from Fiji of the beautiful lady Sina,
And that all the swells of Fiji were running after her.
etc.

82

7. Then off went Sinaleuuna and Sinaeteva to Fiji,
And took with them the shadow of their brother Maluafiti.

etc.

8. The two sisters dressed up and went to tell her
All about their handsome brother.
But they were slighted and shamefully treated by Sina.

etc.

9. Sina did not know they were the sisters of Maluafiti.
She had heard of his beauty and longed for his coming.

etc.

10. The sisters were still ill-treated by Sina; their anger rose,
And off they went to the water where Sina was bathing.
They threw out from the bottle on to the water the shadow of their
    brother.

etc.

11. Sina looked at the shadow and was struck with its beauty.
"That is my husband," said she, "wherever I can find him."

etc.

12. Then Sinaleuuna wept and uttered in soliloquy:
"Oh, Sinaleuuna, Sinaeteva, you are enraged!
Where is our brother? 'Tis for him we are here and slighted."

etc.

13. Sina called out to the villagers for all to come,
All the beautiful young men to assemble and find out
Of whom the figure in the water was the image.

etc.

14. They sought in vain, they could not find.
The shadow was bright and beautiful and compared with no one.
When Maluafiti turned about in his own land,
The shadow wheeled round and round in the water.

etc.

15. But Sina heard not the weeping of the sisters of Maluafiti.
Again their song rang out, "Where is our brother?
'Tis for him we are here and slighted."

etc.

16. "Oh, Maluafiti! rise up, it is day;
Your shadow prolongs our ill-treatment.
Maluafiti come and talk with her face to face,
Instead of that image in water."

etc.

17. Sina had listened, and now she knew 'twas the shadow of Maluafiti.
These are his sisters too, and I've been ill-using them.

etc.

18. Sina reproached herself: "Oh! I fear these ladies;
I knew not they were seeking a wife for their brother Maluafiti.

etc.

19. "Come, oh come," said Sina, "forgive me, I've done you wrong."
Sina begged pardon in vain, the ladies were angry still.

etc.

20. The canoe of Maluafiti arrived.
He came to court Lady Sina, and also to fetch his sisters.

etc.

21. He came, he heard the tale of his sisters,
And then up flew implacable rage.

etc.

22. Sina longed to get Maluafiti;
He was her heart's desire, and long she had waited for him.

etc.

23. Maluafiti frowned and would return,
And off he went with his sisters.
Sina cried and screamed, and determined to follow swimming.

etc.

24. The sisters pleaded to save and to bring her,
Maluafiti relented not, and Sina died in the ocean.

etc.

In a story about another lady called Sinasengi, we are told about her wonderful pool. She had "caught the shadows" of a variety of scenes, and imprinted them on the *water*. A problem this for the photographers! Night-dances, races, club exercise, battles, public meetings, and some of the ordinary employments of daily life were all there. The pool was covered over, but by the removal of a stone this "chamber of imagery" could be all seen. Everything seemed so real that a man one day was so enraptured with the sight of one of his favourite sports that he jumped in to join a dancing party. But, alas! he bruised his head and broke his arm on the *stones* which he found under the surface, instead of the gambols of living men.

Stories also of wifely and husband affection and the reverse are preserved in song. Take the following as a specimen. The original runs through twenty-six verses, but I abbreviate and give the substance:—

There was a youth called Siati noted for his singing. A serenading god came along, threw down a challenge, and promised him his fair daughter if he was the better singer. They sung, Siati beat, and off he went to the land of the god, riding on a shark belonging to his aunt.

They reached the place. The shark went in to the shore, set him down, and told him to go to the bathing-place, where he would find the daughters of the god, the one was called Puapae, "White Fish," and the other Puauli, "Dark Fish."

Siati went and sat down at the bathing-place. The girls had been there, but had gone away. Puapae had forgotten her comb, returned to get it, and there she found Siati. "Siati," said she, "however have you come here?" "I've come to seek the song-god and get his daughter to wife." "My father," said she, "is more of a god than a man—eat nothing he hands you, never sit on a high seat lest death should follow, and now let us unite." Siati and Puapae were united in marriage, but they were sent off to live elsewhere.

The god sent his daughter Puauli to Puapae to tell her husband to build him a house, and that it must be finished that very day, under a penalty of death and the oven. Siati cried, but his wife Puapae comforted him, said she could do it, and off she went and built the house, and by the evening was weeding all around it.

In came another order, and that was for Siati to fight with the dog. The fight took place and Siati conquered. Next the god had lost his ring, and Siati must go to the sea and find it. Again Siati wept, and again his wife cheered him. "I'll find the ring," said she; "only do what I tell you. Cut my body in two, throw me into the sea, and stand still on the beach till I come." He did so, cut her in two, threw her into the sea, she was changed into a fish, and away she went to seek for the ring.

Siati stood, and stood, sat and lay down, stood again, and then lay down, and went off to sleep. Puapae returned, she was thrown up by the fish and stood on the shore. Siati awoke by the splash of the sea on his face. She scolded him for not keeping awake, and then said, "There is the ring, go with it in the early morning," and in the morning off the two went to her father.

That very morning the god called his daughter Puauli and said, "Come, take me on your back, and let us seek Siati that I may eat him." Presently they started back, Siati and Puapae were coming. Puapae and Siati threw down the comb and it became a bush of thorns in the way to intercept the god and Puauli. But they struggled through the thorns. A bottle of earth was next thrown down, and that became a mountain; and then followed their bottle of water, and that became a sea and drowned the god and Puauli.

Puapae said to Siati, "My father and sister are dead, and all on account of my love to you; you may go now and visit your family and friends while I remain here, but see that you do not behave unseemly." He went, visited all his friends, and then he forgot his wife Puapae. He tried to marry again, but Puapae came and stood on the other side. The chief called out, "Which is your wife, Siati?" "The one on the right side." Puapae then broke silence with, "Ah Siati, you have forgotten all I did for you;" and off she went. Siati remembered it all, darted after her crying, and then fell down and died.

CHAPTER VIII.

FOOD—COOKING—LIQUORS.

Animal and Vegetable Food.—Bread-fruit, taro, yams, bananas, and cocoa-nuts formed the staff of life in Samoa. The lagoons and reefs furnish a large supply of fish and shell-fish, of which the natives are very fond; and occasionally all, but especially persons of rank, regaled themselves on pigs, fowls, and turtle. A detailed account of the flora and fauna in this and other groups in Central and Eastern Polynesia will be found in the published volumes of the United States Exploring Squadron of 1838-1842.

Taro, cocoa-nuts, and 'ava were said to have been brought from the heavens by a chief called Losi. When on a visit there he was pleased with the taste of taro, and tried to get some to take down with him. He found a young shoot about the cooking-house, concealed it under his clothing, but the Tangaloans were on the watch. They made him take off his roundabout, snatched the plant from him, pulled his hair, scratched and cut his skin, and back he came to the earth in a great rage.

He engaged six of the gods to go up with him again and be avenged on Tangaloa and his people. He proposed to take up a present of fish. They caught ten, and were up before daybreak, and laid down a fish on the doorstep of ten of the houses. When the people came out of their houses they stumbled over the slippery fish, fell and cut their foreheads. They cooked the fish, but ate it with bruised heads. And hence the proverb in times of difficulty, "To eat with a bruise."

Then followed a number of schemes on the part of the Tangaloans to kill Losi and his party similar to those described (p. 250). But all failed, and then up jumped Losi and his party, and ran at the Tangaloans, who fled and called out as they ran, "What do you want?" "Cocoa-nuts," said Losi. "Take them all," was the reply. Losi again called to his party to *chase*, and they rushed after the Tangaloans, who again shouted back, "What do you want?" "Taro," said Losi, "to compensate for ill usage and the tearing of my skin." "Take it, your claim is just; take it and be off." Losi ordered still to pursue, and again the call came from the frightened Tangaloans, "What else do you want?" "I want 'ava," replied Losi. "Take it, all kinds of it, and be off." Losi conquered, had his revenge, and got what he wanted, and so came down from the heavens with taro, cocoa-nuts, and 'ava, and planted them all about.

For about half the year the Samoans have an abundant supply of food from the bread-fruit trees. During the other half they depend principally on their taro plantations. Bananas and cocoa-nuts are plentiful throughout the year. While the bread-fruit is in season every family lays up a quantity in a pit lined with banana and cocoa-nut leaves, and covered in with stones. It soon ferments; but they keep it in that state for years, and the older it is they relish it all the more. They bake this in the form of little cakes, when the bread-fruit is out of season, and especially when there is a scarcity of taro. The odour of these cakes is offensive in the extreme to a European; but a Samoan turns from a bit of English cheese with far more disgust than we do from his fermented bread-fruit.

A crop of bread-fruit is sometimes shaken off the trees by a gale before it is ripe, and occasionally taro plantations are destroyed by drought and caterpillars; but the people have wild yams in the bush, preserved bread-fruit, cocoa-nuts, and fish to fall back upon; so that there is rarely, if ever, anything like a serious famine. A scarcity of food, occasioned by any of the causes just named, they were in the habit of tracing to the wrath of one of their gods, called *O le Sa* (or the Sacred One). The sun, storms, caterpillars, and all destructive insects were said to be his *au ao*, or servants, who were commissioned to go forth and eat up the plantations of those with whom he was displeased. In times of plenty as well as of scarcity the people were in the habit of assembling with offerings of food, and poured out drink-offerings of 'ava to Le Sa, to propitiate his favour.

A story is told of a woman and her child, who in a time of great scarcity were neglected by the family. One day they cooked some wild yams, but never offered her a share. She was vexed, asked the child to follow her, and when they reached a precipice on the rocky coast, seized the child and jumped over. It is said they were changed into turtles, and afterwards came in that form at the call of the people of the village.

Cannibalism.—During some of their wars, a body was occasionally cooked by the Samoans; but they affirm that, in such a case, it was always some one of the enemy who had been notorious for provocation or cruelty, and that eating a part of his body was considered the climax of hatred and revenge, and was not occasioned by the mere relish for human flesh, such as obtained in the Fiji, New Hebrides, and New Caledonian groups. In more remote heathen times, however, they may have indulged this savage appetite. To speak of roasting him is the very worst language that can be addressed to a Samoan. If applied to a chief of importance, he may raise war to avenge the insult. It is the custom on the submission of one party to another to bow down before their conquerors each with a piece of firewood and a bundle of leaves, such as are used in dressing a pig for the oven; as much as to say, "Kill us and cook us, if you please." Criminals, too, are sometimes bound hand to hand and foot to foot; slung on a pole put through between the hands and feet, carried and laid down before the parties they have injured, like a pig about to be killed and cooked. So deeply humiliating is this act considered that the culprit who consents to degrade himself so far is almost sure to be forgiven.

From such references to cannibalism as we have at pp. 47, 48, and also the following fragments from old stories, it is further apparent that the custom was not unknown in Samoa.

During a great scarcity occasioned by a gale cannibalism prevailed. When a light was wanted in the evening, two or three went to fetch it—it was not safe for one to go alone. If a child was seen out of doors, some one would entice it by holding up something white and calling the child to get a bit of cocoa-nut kernel, and so kidnap and cook.

A story is also told of a woman who had a child who was playing on the surf on the beach. Three of her brothers came along and begged her to let them have the child. She said that if a *bloody* surf should suddenly appear they might have the child, but not otherwise. Presently the surf dashed red and bloody on the shore. She kept to her word, and let the heartless fellows carry off the boy to the oven.

Here is another piece about Ae a Tongan, who attached himself to the Samoan chief Tinilau. Tinilau travelled from place to place on two turtles. Ae wished to visit Tonga, and begged from his master the loan of the turtles. He got them, with the caution to be very careful of them. As soon as he reached Tonga he called his friends to take on shore the turtles, kill them, and have a feast, and this they gladly did.

Tinilau, after waiting long for the return of the turtles, suspected they had been killed. This was confirmed in his mind by the appearance on the beach of a bloody wave. He called a meeting of all the avenging gods of Savaii, and put the case into their hands. They went off to Tonga, found Ae at midnight in a sound sleep, picked him up, brought him back to Samoa, and laid him down in the front room of the house of Tinilau.

At cock-crowing Ae woke up and said aloud, "Why, you cock! you crow like the one belonging to the *pig* I lived with." Tinilau called out from his room, "Had the fellow you lived with such a fowl?" "Yes, the *pig* had one just like it." "Tell us more about him," and so Ae went on chattering, and still using the abusive epithet *pig* when speaking of his master, and talked about the turtles, what a fine feast they had, etc. As it got lighter, he looked up to the roof and said, "This too is just like the house the *pig* lived in." By-and-by he woke up, as it got light, to the full consciousness that somehow or other he was again in the very house of

Tinilau, and that his cannibal master was in the next room. He was dumb and panic-stricken. Orders were given to kill him, and he was despatched accordingly, and his body dressed for the oven. And hence the proverb for any similar action, or if any one takes by mistake or intention what belongs to another, he says in making an apology, "I am like Ae."

Another curious fragment goes from cannibalism to the origin of pigs. A cannibal chief had human victims taken to him regularly, and was in the habit of throwing the heads into a cave close by. A great many heads had been cast in, and he thought no more about them. One day, however, he was sitting on a rock outside the cave when he heard an unusual noise. On looking in, the place was full of *pigs*, and hence the belief that pigs had their origin in the heads of men, or, as some would call it, a humbling case of evolution *downwards*!

Cooking.—The Samoans had and still have, the mode of cooking with hot stones which has been often described as prevailing in the South Sea Islands. Fifty or sixty stones about the size of an orange, heated by kindling a fire under them, form, with the hot ashes, an ordinary oven. The taro, bread-fruit, or yams, are laid among the stones, a thick covering of bread-fruit and banana leaves is laid over all, and in about an hour all is well cooked. In the same oven they bake other things, such as fish, done up in leaves and laid side by side with the taro or other vegetables. Little bundles of taro leaves, too, mixed with the expressed juice of the cocoa-nut kernel, and some other dishes, of which cocoa-nut is generally the chief ingredient, are baked at the same time, and used as a relish in the absence of animal food. Salt water is frequently mixed up with these dishes, which is the only form in which they use salt. They had no salt, and were not in the habit of preserving fish or pork otherwise than by repeated cooking. In this way they kept pork for a week, and fish for three weeks or a month. However large, they cooked the entire pig at once; then, using a piece of split bamboo as a carving-knife, cut it up and divided it among the different branches of the family. The duties of cooking devolved on the men; and all, even chiefs of the highest rank, considered it no disgrace to assist in the cooking-house occasionally.

Forbidden Food.—Some birds and fishes were sacred to particular deities, as has been described, and certain parties abstained from eating them. A man would not eat a fish which was supposed to be under the protection and care of his household god; but he would eat, without scruple, fish sacred to the gods of other families. The dog, and some kinds of fish and birds, were sacred to the greater deities—the *dii majorum gentium* of the Samoans; and, of course, all the people rigidly abstained from these things. For a man to kill and eat anything he considered to be under the special protection of his god, was supposed to be followed by the god's displeasure in the sickness or death of himself, or some member of the family. The same idea seems to have been a check on cannibalism, as there was a fear lest the god of the deceased would be avenged on those who might cook and eat the body.

Liquors.—The young cocoa-nut contains about a tumblerful of a liquid something resembling water sweetened with lump-sugar, and very slightly acid. This is the ordinary beverage of the Samoans. A young cocoa-nut baked in the oven yields a hot draught, which is very pleasant to an invalid. They had no fermented liquors; but they made an intoxicating draught from an infusion of the chewn root of the 'ava plant (*Piper methysticum*). A bowl of this disgustingly-prepared stuff was made and served out when a party of chiefs sat down to a meal. At their ordinary meals few partook of it but the father, or other senior members of the family. It was always taken before, and not after the meal. Among a formal party of chiefs it was handed round in a cocoa-nut shell cup with a good deal of ceremony. When the cup was filled the name, or title rather, of the person for whom it was intended was called out; the cup-bearer took it to him, he received it, drank it off, and returned the cup to be filled again, as the "portion" of another chief. The most important chiefs had the first cups, and, following the order of rank, all had a draught. The liquor was much diluted; few drank to excess; and, upon the whole, the Samoans were perhaps among the most temperate 'ava drinkers in the South Seas. The old men considered that a little of it strengthened them and prolonged life; and often they had a cup the first thing in the morning.

Hospitality.—The Samoans were remarkable for hospitality. Travelling parties never needed to take food for any place beyond the first stage of their journey. Every village had its "large house," kept in good order, and well spread with mats for the reception of strangers. On the arrival of a party some of the members of every family in the village assembled and prepared food for them. It was the province of the head of one particular family to decide, and send word to the rest, how much it would be necessary for each to provide. After all was cooked, it was taken and laid down in front of the house, and, on presenting it, one of them would make a speech, welcoming them to their village; and, although a sumptuous repast had been provided, an apology would be made that there was nothing better. The strangers replied, returned thanks, and exchanged kind words. In the event of there being a chief of high rank among the party, it would probably be decided that every man, woman, and child of the place turn out, dress themselves in their best, walk in single file, each carrying a fish, a fowl, a lobster, a yam, or something else in the hand, and, singing some merry chant as they went along, proceed to the place, and there lay down in a heap what they had provided for their guests. An evening ball or night-dance was also considered an indispensable accompaniment to the entertainment. A travelling party rarely spent more than one night at a place.

Meals.—The Samoans had a meal about 11 A.M., and their principal meal in the evening. At the evening meal every family was assembled; and men, women, and children all ate together. They had no tables, but seated themselves cross-legged round the circular house on mats. Each had his portion laid down before him on a bread-fruit leaf; and thus they partook, in primitive style, without knife, fork, or spoon. Should any strangers be present, due respect was shown to them by laying before them "a worthy portion." After the meal, water to wash was handed round, and a *rub* on the post of the house was the usual table-napkin.

The head of the family, in taking his cup of 'ava at the commencement of the evening meal, would pour out a little of it on the ground, as a drink-offering to the gods, and, all being silent, he would utter aloud the following prayer:—

"Here is 'ava for you, O gods! Look kindly towards this family; let it prosper and increase; and let us all be kept in health. Let our plantations be productive; let fruit grow; and may there be abundance of food for us, your creatures.

"Here is 'ava for you, our war gods! Let there be a strong and numerous people for you in this land.

"Here is 'ava for you, O sailing gods![1] Do not come on shore at this place; but be pleased to depart along the ocean to some other land."

It was also very common to pray with an offering of "flaming fire," just before the evening meal. Calling upon some one to blow up the fire and make it blaze, and begging all to be silent, a senior member of the family would pray aloud as follows:—

"This light is for you, O king[2] and gods superior and inferior! If any of you are forgotten do not be angry, this light is for you all. Be propitious to this family; give life to all; and may your presence be prosperity. Let our children be blessed and multiplied. Remove far from us fines and sicknesses. Regard our poverty; and send us food to eat, and cloth to keep us warm. Drive away from us sailing gods, lest they come and cause disease and death. Protect this family by your presence, and may health and long life be given to us all."

It is related of an old chief in Savaii, that one night at the evening meal he ordered a sea-crab to be reserved for his breakfast. In the night some lads of the family got up and ate it. Next morning the old man was in a great rage, rose, and said to his daughter that he was going off to commit suicide, he could bear no longer the unkindness of the family. He seized his staff and went off to the mountain, where there is a deep ravine. When he reached the edge of the precipice he called to his daughter, who had followed him, that he would jump over, and cause a storm to arise and destroy the place—and over he went. The daughter thought it was of no use to go home, and so she lay down on the edge of the ravine, and became a mountain to shut up the storm and save the people from the threatened wrath of her father.

FOOTNOTES:

1   Gods supposed to come in Tongan canoes and foreign vessels.
2   The principal god of the family.

CHAPTER IX.

CLOTHING.

In our last chapter we alluded to the food of the Samoans, and now proceed to a description of their clothing, the materials of which it is made, their modes of ornament, etc.

During the day a covering of *ti* leaves *(Dracæna terminalis)* was all that either sex thought necessary. "They sewed" *ti* "leaves together, and made themselves aprons." The men had a small one about a foot square, the women had theirs made of longer *ti* leaves, reaching from the waist down below the knee, and made wide, so as to form a girdle covering all round. They had no regular covering for any other part of the body. Occasionally, during rain, they would tie a banana leaf round the head for a cap, or hold one over them as an umbrella. They made shades for the eyes of a little piece of plaited cocoa-nut leaflet; and sometimes they made sandals of the plaited bark of the *Hibiscus tiliaceus*, to protect the feet while fishing among the prickly coral about the reef.

Native Cloth.—At night they slept on a mat, using as a covering a mat or a sheet of native cloth, and inclosed all round by a curtain of the same material to keep out musquitoes. In sickness, also, they wrapped themselves up in native cloth. Their native cloth was made of the inner bark of the paper mulberry *(Morus papyrifera)* beaten out on a board, and joined together with arrow-root, so as to form any width or length of cloth required.

The juice of the raspings of the bark of trees, together with red clay, turmeric, and the soot of burnt candle-nut, furnished them with colouring matter and varnish, with which they daubed their native cloth in the form of squares, stripes, triangles, etc., but, with a few exceptions, perhaps, devoid of taste or regularity.

Tutunga is the native name of the paper mulberry. A fabulous story is told of it and a stinging tree called Salato. As the tale goes, they were two brothers, and had each his plot of ground and a distinct boundary. One morning Tutunga stretched over his boundary and crossed to Salato. Salato was displeased and complained to Tutunga, but he was sullen and made no reply. The affair was referred to the parents; who decided that the two should separate, and that Salato should go further inland, and be sacred and respected; and so it is, no one dares to touch it. On the other hand, Tutunga was severely punished for having proudly crossed his boundary. He was to be cut, and skinned, and beaten, and painted, and made to cover the bodies of men. Then to rot, and then to be burned. And so it is—thus ends Tutunga the proud.

Fine Mats.—Their fine mats were, and are still, considered their most valuable clothing. These mats are made of the leaves of a species of pandanus scraped clean and thin as writing-paper, and slit into strips about the sixteenth part of an inch wide. They are made by the women; and, when completed, are from two to three yards square. They are of a straw and cream colour, are fringed, and, in some instances, ornamented with small scarlet feathers inserted here and there. These mats are thin, and almost as flexible as a piece of calico. Few of the women can make them, and many months—yea, years, are sometimes spent over the making of a single mat. These fine mats are considered their most valuable property, and form a sort of currency which they give and receive in exchange. They value them at from two to forty shillings each. They are preserved with great care; some of them pass through several generations, and as their age and historic interest increase, they are all the more valued.

Another kind of fine mats for clothing they weave out of the bark of a plant of the nettle tribe, which is extensively spread over these islands without any cultivation. They are shaggy on the one side, and, when bleached white, resemble a prepared fleecy sheep-skin. These they sometimes dye with red clay found in the mountains. From the strength and whiteness of the fibre manufactured from this plant, it is capable of being turned to great use.

Cleanliness.—As the native cloth cannot be washed without destroying it, it is generally filthy in the extreme before it is laid aside. This has induced a habit of carelessness in washing cotton and other garments, which is very offensive and difficult to eradicate. They are cleanly, however, in other habits beyond most of the natives of Polynesia. Their floor and sleeping mats are kept clean and tidy. They generally use the juice of the wild orange in cleansing, and bathe regularly every day. It is worth remarking, too, that, while bathing, they have a girdle of leaves or some other covering round the waist. In this delicate sense of propriety it would be well for some more civilised parts of the world to learn a lesson from the Samoans.

Special Occasions.—At marriages and on other gala days, the women, and many of the men, laid aside the leaves and girded themselves with fine mats. Gay young men and women decorated themselves with garlands of flowers or shells. The nautilus shell, broken into small pieces, and strung together, was a favourite head-dress. They oiled themselves from head to foot with scented oil, and sometimes mixed turmeric with the oil to give their skin a tinge of yellow.

Both sexes kept uncovered the upper part of the body, and wore shells, beads, or other trinkets round the neck. They prided themselves also in dressing their children in a similar style. The women wore the hair short, and, on occasions, sometimes had it raised and stiffened with a mixture of scented oil and the gum of the bread-fruit tree. It was fashionable, also, for young women to have a small twisted lock of hair, with a curl at the end of it, hanging from the left temple. The men wore their hair long and gathered up in a knot on the crown of the head, a little to the right side. In company, however, and when attending religious services, they were careful to untie the string, and let their hair flow behind, as a mark of respect. Gay young men occasionally cut their hair short, leaving a small twisted lock hanging down towards the breast from either temple. Their hair is naturally black; but they were fond of dyeing it a light brown colour, by the application of lime, which they made by burning the coral. To dye hair, and also to rub and blind the eyes of pigs which trespassed into neighbouring plantations, were the only uses to which they applied lime in the time of heathenism.

The beard they shaved with the teeth of the shark. Armlets of small white shells were worn by the men above the elbow-joint. Some pierced their ears with a thorn, and wore a small flower for an earring; but this was not very common. A long comb, made from the stem of the cocoa-nut leaflet, was a common ornament of the women, and worn in the hair behind the ear. For a looking-glass, they sometimes used a tub of water; but in arranging the head-dress, they were more frequently guided by the eyes and taste of others. The tattooing, which we described in a previous chapter, was also considered one of their principal ornaments.

There is a story told of a Fijian chief called Fulualela, *Feathers-of-the-Sun*, who came with his daughter to visit Samoa. He had heard of the beauty of the islands and their handsome inhabitants, and thought he might find here a husband chief for his daughter. He was greatly surprised, however, to discover that while the islands were lovely, and the people attractive, they had no mats in their houses, but slept on dried grass like the pigs. He could not think of leaving his daughter; but when he returned to Fiji he made up a present of fine mats, native cloth, and scented oil, as if it were his daughter's dowry, and went back to Samoa with the generous gift, adding also pandanus and paper mulberry plants with which to stock Samoa with material for making such household comforts as mats and native cloth. And hence it is said that ever since the gift of Feathers-of-the-Sun from Fiji, Samoa has had the luxuries of mats to sleep on, and sheets of native cloth to cover them.

CHAPTER X.

AMUSEMENTS.

Under the head of *amusements*, dancing, wrestling, boxing, fencing, and a variety of games and sports, call for description, and to these we shall briefly advert.

Dancing was a common entertainment on festive occasions, such as a marriage. Some of their dances were in the daytime, and, like dress-balls of other countries, were accompanied with a display of fancy mats and other Samoan finery. At the night assemblies the men dressed in their short leaf aprons. Sometimes only the men danced, at other times women, and occasionally the parties were mixed. They danced in parties of two, three, and upwards, on either side. If the one party moved in one direction, the other party took the opposite. They had also various gesticulations, which they practised with some regularity. If, for example, the one party moved along with the right arm raised, the other did precisely the same. It was posturing rather than saltation.

Singing, clapping the hands, beating time on the floor-mats, and drumming, were the usual musical accompaniments. Their music, on these occasions, was a monotonous chant of a line or two, repeated over and over again, with no variety beyond two or three notes. They sought variety rather in *time*. They began slow, and gradually increased until, at the end of ten or twenty minutes, they were full of excitement, the perspiration streaming down, and their tongues galloping over the rhyme at breathless speed. For a drum, they had two or three contrivances. One, a log of wood six or eight feet long, hollowed out from a narrow elongated opening on the upper surface; and this they beat with a short stick or mallet. Another was a set of bamboos, four feet long and downwards, arranged like a Pan's pipe, having the open ends inclosed in a mat bag, and this bag they beat with a stick. A third kind of drumming was effected by four or five men, each with a bamboo open at the top and closed at the bottom, with which, holding vertically, they beat the ground, or a stone or any hard substance, and as the bamboos are of various lengths, they emitted a variety of sounds. At these night-dances all kinds of obscenity in looks, language, and gesture prevailed; and often they danced and revelled till daylight.

Court buffoons furnished some amusement at dancing and other festivals, and also at public meetings. If a chief of importance went to any of these assemblies he had in his train one or two humourists, who, by oddity in dress, gait, or gesture, or by lascivious jokes, tried to excite laughter.

Boxing and fencing were common on festive days, and often led to serious quarrels. In fencing, they used the stalk of the cocoa-nut leaf as a substitute for a club. *Women*, as well as men, entered the ring, and strove for the fame of a pugilist.

Wrestling was another amusement. Sometimes they chose sides, say four against four; and the party who had the most thrown had to furnish their opponents with a cooked pig, served up with taro, or supply any other kind of food that might be staked at the outset of the game. A supply of some kind of food was the usual forfeit in all their games.

Clasp and undo was another kind of wrestling. One man clasped a second tightly round the waist, and this second does the same to a third. The three thus fastened together lay down and challenged any single man to separate them. If he succeeded, they paid the forfeit; if not, he did.

Throwing the spear was also common. The young men of one street or village matched against those of another; and, after fixing a mark in the distance, threw a small wooden javelin so that it might first strike the ground, and then spring upwards and onwards in the direction of the mark. They who threw farthest won the game, and had a repast of food at the expense of those who lost it. In more direct spear-throwing they set up the stem of a young cocoa-nut tree, with the base upwards, which is soft and spongy. One party threw at it, and filled it with spears. The other party threw, and tried to knock them down. If any remained after all had thrown they were counted until they reached the number fixed for the game. In another of these amusements a man stood in the distance and allowed another to throw spears at him. He had no shield, but merely a club; and with this he showed surprising dexterity in hitting off spear after spear as it approached him.

Fishing matches were in vogue at particular seasons. The party who took the most fish won, and were treated with cooked pigs and other viands by those who lost.

Pigeon-catching was another amusement, and one, like our English falconry of other days, in which the chiefs especially delighted. The principal season set in about June. Great preparations were made for it; all the pigs of a settlement were sometimes slaughtered and baked for the occasion; and, laden with all kinds of food, the whole population of the place went off to certain pigeon-grounds in the bush. There they put up huts, and remained sometimes for months at the sport.

The ground being cleared, the chiefs stationed themselves at distances all round a large circular space, each concealed under a low shed or covering of brushwood, having by his side a net attached to a long bamboo, and in his hand a stick with a tame pigeon on a crook at the end of it. This pigeon was trained to fly round and round, as directed by its owner, with a string at its foot thirty feet long, attached to the end of his stick. Every man flew his pigeon, and then the whole circle looked like a place where pigeons were flocking round food or water. The scene soon attracted some wild pigeon; and, as it approached the spot, whoever was next to it raised his net and tried to entangle it. He who got the greatest number of pigeons was the hero of the day, and honoured by his friends with various kinds of food, with which he treated his less successful competitors. Some of the pigeons were baked, others were distributed about and tamed for further use. Taming and exercising them for the sporting season was a common pastime.

Spinning the cocoa-nut was another amusement. A party sat down in a circle, and one in the centre spinned a cocoa-nut. When it rested they saw to whom the three black marks or eyes on the end of the shell pointed, and imposed upon him some little service to the whole, such as unhusking chestnuts, or going for a load of cocoa-nuts. This is especially worthy of remark, as it was the Samoan method of *casting lots*. If a number of people were unwilling to go a message or do a piece of work, they decided the matter by wheeling round the cocoa-nut to see to whom it turned its *face*, as they called it, when it rested. Sometimes they appealed to this lot, and fixed the charge of stealing on a person towards whom the *face* of the cocoa-nut pointed.

They had also a game of *hide-and-seek*, with the addition that those who hid tried to escape those who sought, and ran to a given post or mark. All who reached the post were counted towards making up the game.

Pitching small cocoa-nut shells to the end of a mat was a favourite amusement of the chiefs. They tried to knock each other's shells off the given spot. They played in parties of two and two, with five shells each. They who had most shells left on the place after all had thrown won.

They had also *guessing* sports. One party hid, the other bundled up one of their number in a large basket covered over with a mat or cloth. Then they too hid, all but three, who carried the basket to the other party for them to guess who was in it. If they guessed correctly, then they in turn got the basket to do the same. The successful guesses were counted for the game.

They were in the habit of amusing themselves with *riddles*, of which the following are a specimen:—

"1.   A man who continues standing out of doors with a burden on his back.—*Explanation*. A banana tree, with a bunch of bananas.

"2.   There are twenty brothers, each with a hat on his head.—*Explan*. A man's fingers and toes; the nails of which are represented as hats.

"3.   A man who stands between two ravenous fish.—*Explan*. The tongue, as being placed between the teeth of the upper and lower jaws.

"4.   There are four brothers, who are always bearing about their father.—*Explan*. The Samoan pillow, formed by four legs and a bamboo; the legs being the four brothers, the bamboo the father.

"5.   There is a man who calls out continually day and night.—*Explan*. The surf on the reef, which never rests.

"6.   There is a man who, when he leaves the bush, is very little; but when he has reached the sea-shore, becomes very great.—*Explan*. The bark of the paper-mulberry, which, when first taken off the wood, is very narrow; but, when beaten out to make the native cloth, becomes very broad.

"7.   A man who has a white head stands above the fence, and reaches to the heavens.—*Explan*. The smoke rising from the oven.

"8.   The person who sleeps on a bed of whales' teeth.—*Explan*. A fowl sitting on her eggs.

"9.   Many brothers, but only one intestine.—*Explan*. A string of beads. The beads being the brothers, and the string the intestine.

"10.   A long house with one post.—*Explan*. The nose; the septum being the post."

They had also games at *rhyming*. One party would choose the names of trees and another the names of men. Those who sided with the trees would say: "There is the *Fau* tree, tell us a name which will rhyme with it." The reply would perhaps be *Tulifau*.

Again, there is the *Toa*, and the other party would reply *Tuisamoa*. And so on they went till one party had exhausted all the names they could think of, owned the defeat, and paid the forfeit.

In a similar game one party would name a bird or beast, and the other a fish with a corresponding rhyme. For example, for the birds:

Lupe,	they would give the name of the fish, Une.
Ngongo,	Do. do. do. Alongo.
Tiotala,	Do. do. do. Ngatala.

Here, too, there was a forfeit if beaten. They had *tripping and stammering* games also. One party would say to the other—you repeat

"O lo matou niu afaafa lava le la i tuafale,
Sasa, ma fili, ma faataa, ma lafo i fongavai."

If any one tripped when repeating it he had to pay a forfeit.
Another might be in rhyme and run as follows:

"Na au sau mai Safata,
Ou afe i le ngatai ala,
E fafanga i si au tiaa,
Fafanga, fafanga, pa le manava.
Fafanga, fafanga, pa le manava."

Another as his puzzle to repeat correctly would give:

"Na au sau mai Mali'oli'o,
Lou ala i umu,
Lou ala i paito,

Lou ala i puto pute,
Lou ala i pute puto."

If any one slipped in repeating he paid the forfeit.

In some of their evening sports *theatricals* were in vogue. Illustrations would be given of selfish schemes to take things easy at the expense of others, clownish processions to create laughter, or marriage ceremonies in which, when it came to the point, the bride rebelled and would not have her husband. Ventriloquism also was attempted, in which, as they say, "voices spoke to them without bodies."

They amused each other also by stories of *hoodwinking and trickery*, such as the following:—A Samoan and a Tongan made friends with each other. When the latter went away on a visit to Tonga the former begged him to bring back one of their large cocoa-nuts, which are prized as water-bottles. He promised to do it on condition that the Samoan would look out for him a fine white fowl.

The Samoan got ready the fowl, and made a basket in which to put it. The Tongan returned with a large unhusked nut, but on the voyage he split up the husk, took out the nut, and closed all up again. The Samoan had the gift of *second sight*, knew what the Tongan had done, and so he let loose the white fowl, and put an *owl* in its place in the basket.

The Tongan on his arrival gave him the large *mock* nut, *minus* the real nut and kernel, and the Samoan handed him the basket with the pretended white fowl.

The Tongan jumped into his canoe again, and went off in high glee singing:

"Niu niu, pulu!
Niu niu, pulu!"

"Cocoa-nut, cocoa-nut,
Only a *husk*!"

But the wind was taken out of his sail by the laughter and antics of his friend on the beach shouting after him:

"Moa, moa, lulu!"
"Fowl, fowl, only an *owl*!"

They had *sundry other amusements*. Swimming in the surf on a board, and steering little canoes while borne along on the crest of a wave towards the shore, were favourite juvenile sports. Canoe-racing, races with one party in a canoe and another along the beach, races with both parties on land, climbing cocoa-nut trees to see who can go up quickest, reviews and sham-fighting, cock-fighting, tossing up oranges and keeping three, four, or more of them on the move: these and many other things were of old and are still numbered among Samoan sports. The teeth and jaws, too, are called into exercise. One man would engage to unhusk with his teeth and eat five large native chesnuts (*Tuscapus edulis*) before another could run a certain distance and return. If he failed, he paid his basket of cocoa-nuts, or whatever might be previously agreed upon.

Our juvenile friends will be sure to recognise some of their favourite amusements in this description, and will, perhaps, feel inclined to try the novelty of some of these Samoan variations. What a surprising unity of thought and feeling is discoverable among the various races of mankind from a comparison of such customs as these!

CHAPTER XI.

MORTALITY, LONGEVITY, DISEASES, ETC.

Mortality, longevity, diseases, and the treatment of the sick, will now form the subject of a few observations; and here we begin with—

Infants.—Before the introduction of Christianity probably not less than two-thirds of the Samoan race died in infancy and childhood. This mortality arose principally from carelessness and mismanagement in nursing; evils which still prevail to a great extent. Even now, perhaps, one-half of them die before they reach their second year. The poor little things are often carried about with their bare heads exposed to the scorching rays of a vertical sun. Exposure to the night-damps also, and above all stuffing them with improper food, are evils which often make us wonder that the mortality among them is not greater than it is. The Samoans were always fond of their children, and would have done anything for them when ill; but, with the exception of external applications for skin diseases, they had no proper remedies for the numerous disorders of children. Were their care in preventing disease equal to their anxiety to observe a cure when the child is really ill, there would probably be less sickness among them, and fewer deaths.

Adults.—The universal opinion of the natives is that the mortality is now greater among young and middle-aged people than it was formerly. "It was common," they say, "to see three or four old men in a house, whereas you rarely see more than one now." Among a people destitute of statistics or records of any kind, it is difficult to speak correctly of an earlier date than 1830. Since that time, however, the population has been remarkably stationary. We have not observed any marked disproportion in the deaths of adults of any particular age compared with other parts of the world. A person died in 1847 who was present at the massacre of M. de Langle and others connected with the exploring expedition of La Perouse in 1787, and who was then a youth of about fourteen years of age. Judging from his appearance, we may suppose that there are some in every village who must be sixty, seventy, and even eighty years of age.

They have stories of a *giant race*, and tell particularly of one called *Tafai*. He was very tall and strong, but not cruel to any one. He could throw a long cocoa-nut tree at the rocks as if he were but hurling a thin spear. He plucked up by the roots a great Malili tree, eighty feet high, carried it off on his shoulder, branches and all, and could throw it up and catch it again as if he were playing with a small crab. It is said, too, that so great was his weight, if he put his foot on a rock it left a footprint as if the rock had been soft sand.

Diseases.—Pulmonary affections, paralysis, diseases of the spine producing humpback, ophthalmia, skin diseases, scrofulous, and other ulcers, elephantiasis, and a species of leprosy, are among the principal diseases with which they were afflicted. Ophthalmia and various diseases of the eye were very prevalent. There were few cases of total blindness; but many had one of the organs of vision destroyed. Connected with diseases of the eye, pterygium is common; not only single, but double, triple, and even quadruple are occasionally met with. The leprosy of which we speak has greatly abated. The natives say that formerly many had it, and suffered from its ulcerous sores until all the fingers of a hand or the toes of a foot had fallen off. Elephantiasis, producing great enlargement of the legs and arms, has, they think, somewhat abated too; only, they say, it prevails among the *young* men more now than it did formerly. Insanity is occasionally met with. It was invariably traced in former times to the immediate presence of an evil spirit. If furious, the party was tied hand to hand and foot to foot until a change for the better appeared. Idiots are not common. Consumption they call "Moomoo;" and there were certain native doctors who were supposed to be successful in spearing the disease, or rather the spirit causing it. The doctor when sent for would come in, sit down before the patient, and chant as follows:—

"Moomoo e! Moomoo e!
O le â ou velosia atu oe;"

which in English is—

"O Moomoo! O Moomoo!
I'm on the eve of spearing you."

Then he would rise up, flourish about with his spear over the head of the patient, and leave the house. No one dared speak or smile during the ceremony. Influenza is a new disease to the natives. They say that the first attack of it ever known in Samoa was during the Aana war in 1830, just as the missionaries Williams and Barff, with Tahitian teachers, first reached their shores. The natives at once traced the disease to the foreigners and the new religion; the same opinion spread through these seas, and especially among the islands of the New Hebrides. Ever since there have been returns of the disease almost annually. It is generally preceded by unsettled weather, and westerly or southerly winds. Its course is generally from east to west. It lasts for about a month, and passes off as fine weather and steady trade-winds set in. In many cases it is fatal to old people and those who have been previously weakened by pulmonary diseases. There was an attack in May 1837, and another in November 1846, both of which were unusually severe and fatal. They have a tradition of an epidemic, answering the description of cholera, which raged with fearful violence probably about eighty years ago. In 1849 hooping-cough made its appearance, and prevailed for several months, among adults as well as children. A good many of the children died. In 1851 another new disease surprised the natives—viz. the mumps. It was traced to a vessel from California collecting pigs, and soon spread all over the group. Scarcely a native escaped. It answered the usual description of the attack given in medical works, and passed off in ten days or a fortnight. Hitherto they have been exempt from small-pox. Some years ago the missionaries vaccinated all the natives, and continue to do so as often as a supply of vaccine lymph is obtained.

Medicine.—The Samoans in their heathenism seldom had recourse to any internal remedy except an emetic, which they used after having eaten a poisonous fish. Sometimes juices from the bush were tried; at other times the patient drank on at water until it was rejected; and, on some occasions, mud, and even the most unmentionable filth, was mixed up and taken as an emetic draught. Latterly, as their intercourse with Tongans, Fijians, Tahitians, and Sandwich Islanders increased, they made additions to their *pharmacopœia* of juices from the bush. Each disease had its particular physician. Shampooing and anointing the affected part of the body with scented oil by the native doctors was common; and to this charms were frequently added, consisting of some flowers from the bush done up in a piece of native cloth and put in a conspicuous place in the thatch over the patient.

The advocates of *kinnesipathy* would be interested in finding, were they to visit the South Seas, that most of their friction, percussion, and other manipulations, were in vogue there ages ago, and are still practised. Now, however, European medicines are eagerly sought after; so much so, that every missionary is obliged to have a dispensary, and to set apart a certain hour every day to give advice and medicine to the sick.

As the Samoans supposed disease to be occasioned by the wrath of some particular deity, their principal desire, in any difficult case, was not for medicine, but to ascertain the cause of the calamity. The friends of the sick went to the high priest of the village. He was sure to assign some cause; and, whatever that was, they were all anxiety to have it removed, as the means of restoration. If he said they were to give up a canoe to the god, it was given up. If a piece of land was asked, it was passed over at once. Or, if he did not wish anything particular from the party, he would probably tell them to assemble the family, "confess, and throw out." In this ceremony each member of the family confessed his crimes and any judgments which, in anger, he had invoked on the family or upon the particular member of it then ill; and, as a proof that he revoked all such imprecations, he took a little water in his mouth, and spurted it out towards the person who was sick.

In *surgery*, they lanced ulcers with a shell or a shark's tooth, and, in a similar way, bled from the arm. For inflammatory swellings they sometimes tried local bleeding; but shampooing and rubbing with oil were the more common remedies in such cases. Cuts they washed in the sea, and bound up with a leaf. Into wounds in the scalp they blew the smoke of burnt chestnut wood. To take a barbed spear from the arm or leg they cut into the limb from the opposite side and pushed it right through. Amputation they never attempted.

The *treatment of the sick* was invariably humane, and all that could be expected. They wanted for no kind of food which they might desire, night or day, if it was at all in the power of their friends to procure it. In the event of the disease assuming a dangerous form, messengers were despatched to friends at a distance that they might have an opportunity of being in time to see and say farewell to a departing relative. The greater the rank the greater the stir and muster about the sick of friends from the neighbourhood and from a distance. Every one who went to visit a sick friend supposed to be near death took with him a present of a fine mat, or some other kind of valuable property, as a farewell expression of regard, to aid in paying native doctors or conjurors, and to help also in the cost of pigs, etc., with which to entertain the friends who were assembled. The following story illustrates the ideas and doings of the people at such a time:—

Tuitopetope and Tuioleole were two brother conjurors belonging to Upolu who had been on a visit to Tutuila. On their return they landed at night at Aleipata just as messengers were running from place to place to inform the friends of the dangerous illness of the chief Puepuemai. The two looked into the house, and there they saw a number of gods from the mountain called Fiso sitting in the doorway. They were handing from one to another the soul of the dying chief. It was wrapped up in a leaf, and had been passed by the gods inside the house to those sitting in the doorway. One of them said to Tuitopetope, "You take this," and handed the soul to him. He took it. The god mistook him in the dark for another of their god party. Then all the gods went off, but Tuitopetope remained in the village and kept the soul of the chief.

Next morning some women of the family were sent off with a present of fine mats to fetch a noted priest doctor. Tuitopetope and his brother, who were sitting on the beach as they passed along, asked where they were going with that bundle of property. "To fetch a doctor to Puepuemai," was the reply. "Leave it here," said they, "and take *us*." "Lads! you are joking," said the women. "No, we are not; *we* can heal him." The women went back to the house to consult again with the friends assembled around the dying man. All agreed to let the young men come and do what they could.

Tuitopetope and his brother were accordingly sent for. The chief was very ill, his jaw hanging down, and apparently breathing his last. They undid the leaf, let the soul into him again, and immediately he brightened up and lived. It was blazed abroad that Puepuemai was brought to life again by Tuitopetope and his brother, and they gained a wonderful celebrity. It was supposed they knew everything and could do anything; and so they were sent for by chiefs all over the group to heal the sick and find out the guilty in thieving and other criminalities.

CHAPTER XII.

DEATH AND BURIAL.

Whenever the eye was fixed in death the house became a scene of indescribable lamentation and wailing. "Oh, my father, why did you not let me die, and you live here still?" "Oh, my brother, why have you run away and left your only brother to be trampled upon?" "Oh, my child, had I known you were going to die! Of what use is it for me to survive you; would that I had died for you!" These and other doleful cries might have been heard two hundred yards from the house; and they were accompanied by the most frantic expressions of grief, such as rending garments, tearing the hair, thumping the face and eyes, burning the body with small piercing firebrands, beating the head with stones till the blood ran, and this they called an "offering of blood" for the dead.

After an hour or so the more boisterous wailing subsided, and, as in such a climate the corpse must be buried in a few hours, preparations were made without delay. The body was laid out on a mat, oiled with scented oil, and, to modify the cadaverous look, they tinged the oil for the face with a little turmeric. The body was then wound up with several folds of native cloth, the chin propped up with a little bundle of the same material, and the face and head left uncovered, while, for some hours longer, the body was surrounded by weeping relatives. If the person had died of a complaint which carried off some other members of the family, they would probably open the body to "search for the disease." Any inflamed substance they happened to find they took away and burned, thinking that this would prevent any other members of the family being affected with the same disease. This was done when the body was laid in the grave.

While a dead body was in the house no food was eaten under the same roof; the family had their meals outside, or in another house. Those who attended the deceased were most careful not to handle food, and for days were fed by others as if they were helpless infants. Baldness and the loss of teeth were supposed to be the punishment inflicted by the household god if they violated the rule. Fasting was common at such times, and they who did so ate nothing during the day, but had a meal in the evening. The fifth day was a day of "purification." They bathed the face and hands with hot water, and then they were "clean," and resumed the usual time and mode of eating.

The death of a chief of high rank was attended with great excitement and display; all work was suspended in the settlement; no stranger dared to pass through the place. For days they kept the body unburied, until all the different parties connected with that particular clan assembled from various parts of the islands, and until each party had, in turn, paraded the body, shoulder high, through the village, singing at the same time some mournful dirge. The body, too, was wrapped up in the most valuable fine mat clothing which the deceased possessed.

The burial generally took place the day after death. As many of the friends as could be present in time attended. Every one brought a present, and the day after the funeral these presents were all so distributed again as that every one went away with something in return for what he brought. The body was buried without a coffin, except in the case of chiefs, when a log of wood was hollowed out for the purpose. The body being put into this rude encasement, all was done up again in some other folds of native cloth, and carried on the shoulders of four or five men to the grave. The friends followed, but in no particular order; and at the grave again there was often further wailing and exclamations, such as, "Alas! I looked to you for protection, but you have gone away; why did you die? would that I had died for you!"

116

The grave was called "the fast resting-place," and in the case of chiefs, "the house thatched with the leaves of the sandal wood," alluding to the custom of planting some tree with pretty foliage near the grave. There was no village burying-ground all preferred laying their dead among the ashes of their ancestors on their own particular ground. They carried the skulls of their dead from a land where they had been residing during war back to the graves of their fathers as soon as possible after peace was proclaimed. The grave was often dug close by the house. They made it about four feet deep, and after spreading it with mats, like a comfortable bed, there they placed the body with the head to the rising of the sun, and the feet to the west. With the body they deposited several things which may have been used during the person's illness, such as his clothing, his drinking-cup, and his bamboo pillow. The sticks used to answer the purpose of a pick-axe in digging the grave were also carefully buried with the body. Not that they thought these things of use to the dead; but it was supposed that if they were left and handled by others further disease and death would be the consequence. Other mats were spread over the body, on these a layer of white sand from the beach, and then they filled up the grave. The spot was marked by a little heap of stones a foot or two high. The grave of a chief was neatly built up in an oblong slanting form, about three feet high at the foot and four at the head. White stones or shells were intermixed with the top layer, and if it had been a noted warrior his grave might be surrounded with spears, or his club laid loosely on the top.

Embalming was known and practised with surprising skill in one particular family of chiefs. Unlike the Egyptian method, as described by Herodotus, it was performed in Samoa exclusively by women. The viscera being removed and buried, they, day after day, anointed the body with a mixture of oil and aromatic juices. To let the fluids escape, they continued to puncture the body all over with fine needles. In about two months the process of desiccation was completed. The hair, which had been cut and laid aside at the commencement of the operation, was now glued carefully on to the scalp by a resin from the bush. The abdomen was filled up with folds of native cloth; the body was wrapped up with the same material, and laid out on a mat, leaving the hands, face, and head exposed. A house was built for the purpose, and there the body was placed with a sheet of native cloth loosely thrown over it. Now and then the face was oiled with a mixture of scented oil and turmeric, and passing strangers were freely admitted to see the remains of the departed. Until about twenty years ago there were four bodies laid out in this way in a house belonging to the family to which we refer, viz. a chief, his wife, and two sons. They were laid on a platform raised on a double canoe. They must have been embalmed upwards of thirty years, and although thus exposed, they were in a remarkable state of preservation. They assigned no particular reason for this embalming, further than that it was the expression of their affection to keep the bodies of the departed still with them as if they were alive. None were allowed to dress them but a particular family of old ladies, who all died off; and, as there was a superstitious fear on the part of some, and an unwillingness on the part of others, to handle them, it was resolved at last to lay them underground.

Burnings for the dead.—On the evening after the burial of any important chief his friends kindled a number of fires at distances of some twenty feet from each other, near the grave; and there they sat and kept them burning till morning light. This was continued sometimes for ten days after the funeral; it was also done before burial. In the house where the body lay, or out in front of it, fires were kept burning all night by the immediate relatives of the departed. The common people had a similar custom. After burial they kept a fire blazing in the house all night, and had the space between the house and the grave so cleared as that a stream of light went forth all night from the fire to the grave. The account the Samoans give of it is, that it was merely a light burning in honour of the departed, and a mark of tender regard.

The unburied occasioned great concern. No Roman was ever more grieved at the thought of his unburied friend wandering a hundred years along the banks of the Styx than were the Samoans while they thought of the spirit of one who had been drowned, or of another who had fallen in war, wandering about neglected and comfortless. They supposed the spirit haunted them everywhere, night and day, and imagined they heard it calling upon them in a most pitiful tone, and saying, "Oh, how cold! oh, how cold!" Nor were the Samoans, like the ancient Romans, satisfied with a mere "*tumulus inanis*" at which to observe the usual solemnities; they thought it was possible to obtain the soul of the departed in some tangible transmigrated form. On the beach, near where a person had been drowned, and whose body was supposed to have become a porpoise, or on the battlefield, where another fell, might have been seen, sitting in silence, a group of five or six, and one a few yards before them with a sheet of native cloth spread out on the ground in front of him. Addressing some god of the family he said, "Oh, be kind to us; let us obtain without difficulty the spirit of the young man!" The first thing that happened to light upon the sheet was supposed to be the spirit. If nothing came it was supposed that the spirit had some ill-will to the person praying. That person after a time retired, and another stepped forward, addressed some other god, and waited the result. By-and-by something came; grasshopper, butterfly, ant, or whatever else it might be, it was carefully wrapped up, taken to the family, the friends assembled, and the bundle buried with all due ceremony, as if it contained the real spirit of the departed. The grave, however, was not the hades of the Samoans, as we have already seen in Chapter II. Prayers at the grave of a parent or brother or *chief* were common. Some, for example, would pray for health in sickness and might or might not recover. A woman prayed for the death of her brother, he died, but soon after she died also. A chief promised to give a woman some fine mats, he deceived her, and off she went and prayed at the grave of his predecessor in the title. The man took ill and died. She confessed what she had done, but said she did not pray for death, but only *pain* to make him smart for his deceit. And so the custom was carried on, but with fluctuating belief in its efficacy.

CHAPTER XIII.

HOUSES.

The Samoans have a tradition that of old their forefathers had no houses. They say that in those days the people were "housed by the heavens," and describe the ingenuity of a chief who first contrived to build houses. He had two sons, and out of love to them built for each of them a house. But leaving tradition let me describe the houses to be seen at the present day in some of the villages, and the counterpart of those which have been in use for ages. Imagine a gigantic bee-hive, thirty-five feet in diameter, a hundred in circumference, and raised from the ground by a number of short posts, at intervals of four feet from each other all round, and you have a good idea of the appearance of a Samoan house.

The spaces between these posts, which may be called open doors or windows all round the house, are shut in at night by roughly-plaited cocoa-nut leaf blinds. During the day the blinds are pulled up, and all the interior exposed to a free current of air. The floor is raised six or eight inches with rough stones, then an upper layer of smooth pebbles, then some cocoa-nut leaf mats, and then a layer of finer matting. Houses of important chiefs are erected on a raised platform of stones three feet high. In the centre of the house there are two, and sometimes three, posts or pillars, twenty feet long, sunk three feet into the ground, and extending to and supporting the ridge pole. These are the main props of the building. Any *Samson* or giant *Tafai* pulling them away would bring down the whole house. The space between the rafters is filled up with what they call *ribs*—viz. the wood of the bread-fruit tree, split up into small pieces, and joined together so as to form a long rod the thickness of the thumb, running from the ridge pole down to the eaves. All are kept in their places, an inch and a half apart, by cross pieces, made fast with cinnet. The whole of this upper cagelike work looks compact and tidy, and at the first glance is admired by strangers as being alike novel, ingenious, and neat. The wood of the bread-fruit tree, of which the greater part of the best houses are built, is durable, and, if preserved from wet, will last fifty years.

The thatch also is laid on with great care and taste; the long dry leaves of the sugar-cane are strung on to pieces of reed five feet long; they are made fast to the reed by overlapping the one end of the leaf, and pinning it with the rib of the cocoa-nut leaflet run through from leaf to leaf horizontally. These reeds, thus fringed with the sugar-cane leaves hanging down three or four feet, are laid on, beginning at the eaves and running up to the ridge pole, each one overlapping its fellow an inch or so, and made fast one by one with cinnet to the inside rods or rafters. Upwards of a hundred of these reeds of thatch will be required for a single row running from the eaves to the ridge pole; then they do another row, and so on all round the house. Two, three, or four thousand of these fringed reeds may be required for a good-sized house. This thatching, if well done, will last for seven years. To collect the sugar-cane leaves, and "sew," as it is called, the ends on to the reeds, is the work of the women. An active woman will sew fifty reeds in a day, and three men will put up and fasten on to the roof of the house some five hundred in a day. Corrugated iron, shingles, and other contrivances, are being tried by European residents; but, for coolness and ventilation, nothing beats the thatch. The great drawback is, that in gales it stands up like a field of corn, and then the rain pours into the house. That, however, may be remedied by a network of cinnet, to keep down the thatch, or by the native plan of covering all in with a layer of heavy cocoa-nut leaves on the approach of a gale.

These great circular roofs are so constructed that they can be lifted bodily off the posts, and removed anywhere, either by land, or by a raft of canoes. But in removing a house, they generally divide the roof into four parts—viz. the two sides, and the two ends, where there are particular joints left by the carpenters, which can easily be untied, and again fastened. There is not a single nail in the whole building; all is made fast with cinnet. As Samoan houses often form presents, fines, dowries, as well as articles of barter, they are frequently removed from place to place. The arrangement of the houses in a village has no regard whatever to order. You rarely see three houses in a line. Every one puts his house on his little plot of ground, just as the shade of the trees, the direction of the wind, the height of the ground, etc., may suit his fancy.

A house, after the usual Samoan fashion just described, has but *one* apartment. It is the common parlour, dining-room, etc., by day, and the bedroom of the whole family by night. They do not, however, altogether herd indiscriminately. If you peep into a Samoan house at midnight, you will see five or six low oblong *tents* pitched (or rather strung up) here and there throughout the house. They are made of native cloth, five feet high, and close all round down to the mat. They shut out the mosquitoes, and enclose a place some eight feet by five; and these said tent-looking places may be called the *bedrooms* of the family. Four or five mats laid loosely, the one on the top of the other, form the *bed*. The *pillow* is a piece of thick bamboo, three inches in diameter, three to five feet long, and raised three inches from the mat by short wooden feet. The sick are indulged with something softer, but the hard bamboo is the invariable pillow of health. The *bedding* in old times was complete with a single mat or sheet of native cloth. In the morning the tent was unstrung, mats, pillow, and sheet rolled together, and laid up overhead on a shelf between the posts in the middle of the house.

These rolls of mats and bedding, a bundle or two done up in native cloth on the same shelf in the centre of the house, a basket, a fan or two, and a bamboo knife stuck into the thatch within reach, a fishing-net, a club, and some spears strung up along the rafters, a few paddles, and a few cocoa-nut shell water-bottles, were about all the things in the shape of furniture or property to be seen in looking into a Samoan house. The fire-place was about the middle of the house. It was merely a circular hollow, two or three feet in diameter, a few inches deep, and lined with hardened clay. It was not used for cooking, but for the purpose of lighting up the house at night. A *flaming fire*, as we have already remarked (p. 75), was the regular evening offering to the gods, as the family bowed the head, and the fathers prayed for prosperity from the "gods great and small." The women collected during the day a supply of dried cocoa-nut leaves, etc., which, with a little management, kept up a continued blaze in the evening, while the assembled family group had their supper and prayer, and sat together chatting for an hour or two afterwards.

But about *house-building*: it was a distinct trade in Samoa; and perhaps, on an average, you might find one among every three hundred men who was a master carpenter. Whenever this person went to work he had in his train some ten or twelve, who followed him, some as journeymen, who expected payment from him, and others as apprentices, who were principally anxious to learn the trade. When a young man took a fancy to the trade he had only to go and attach himself to the staff of some master carpenter, follow him from place to place for a few years, until he thought he could take the lead in building a house himself; and whenever he could point to a house which he had built, that set him up as a professed carpenter, and he would from that time be employed by others.

If a person wished a house built, he went with a fine mat, worth in modern cash value 20s. or 30s. He told the carpenter what he wanted, and presented him with the mat as a pledge that he should be well paid for his work. If he accepted the mat, that was a pledge that he undertook the job. Nothing was stipulated as to the cost; that was left entirely to the honour of the employing party. At an appointed time the carpenter came with his staff of helpers and learners. Even now their only tools are a felling-axe, a hatchet, and a small adze; and there they sit, chop, chop, chopping, for three, six, or nine months it may be, until the house is finished. Their *adze* reminds us of ancient Egypt. It is formed by the head of a small hatchet, or any other flat piece of iron, lashed on, at an angle of forty-five, to the end of a small piece of wood, eighteen inches long, as its handle. Of old they used stone and shell axes and adzes.

The man whose house is being built provides the carpenters with board and lodging, and is also at hand with his neighbours to help in bringing wood from the bush, scaffolding, and other heavy work. As we have just remarked, a Samoan house-builder made no definite charge, but left the price of his work to the judgment, generosity, and means of the person who employed him. It was a lasting disgrace to any one to have it said that he paid his carpenter shabbily. It branded him as a person of no rank or respectability, and was disreputable, not merely to himself, but to the whole family or *clan* with which he was connected. The entire tribe or clan was his *bank*. Being connected with that particular tribe, either by birth or marriage, gave him a latent interest in all their property, and entitled him to go freely to any of his friends to ask for help in paying his house-builder. He would get a mat from one, worth twenty shillings; from another he might get one more valuable still; from another some native cloth, worth five shillings; from another, some foreign property; and thus he might collect, with but little trouble, two or three hundred useful articles, worth, perhaps, forty or fifty pounds; and in this way the carpenter was generally well paid. Now and then there might be a stingy exception; but the carpenter, from certain indications, generally saw ahead, and decamped, with all his party, leaving the house unfinished. It was a standing custom, that after the sides and one end of the house were finished, the principal part of the payment was made; and it was at this time that a carpenter, if he was dissatisfied, would get up and walk off. A house with two sides and but one end, and the carpenters away, was indicative. Nor could the chief to whom the house belonged employ another party to finish it. It was a fixed rule of the trade, and rigidly adhered to, that no one would take up the work which another party had thrown down. The chief, therefore, had no alternative but to go and make up matters with the original carpenter, in order to have his house decently completed. When a house was finished, and all ready for occupation, they had their "house-warming," or, as they called it, its *oven consecration*; and formerly it was the custom to add on to that a night dance, for the purpose, they said, of "treading down the beetles."

The system of a common interest in each other's property, to which we have referred, is still clung to by the Samoans with great tenacity. They feel its advantages when they wish to raise a little. Not only a house, but also a canoe, a boat, a fine, a dowry, and everything else requiring an extra effort, is got up in the same way. They consider themselves at liberty to go and take up their abode anywhere among their friends, and remain without charge, as long as they please. And the same custom entitles them to beg and borrow from each other to any extent. Boats, tools, garments, money, etc., are all freely lent to each other, if connected with the same tribe or clan. A man cannot bear to be called stingy or disobliging. If he has what is asked, he will either give it, or adopt the worse course of telling a lie about it, by saying that he has it not, or that it is promised to some one else. This communistic system is a sad hindrance to the industrious, and eats like a canker-worm at the roots of individual or national progress. No matter how hard a young man may be disposed to work, he cannot keep his earnings: all soon passes out of his hands into the common circulating currency of the clan to which all have a latent right. The only thing which reconciles one to bear with it until it gives place to the individual independence of more advanced civilisation, is the fact that, with such a state of things, no "poor laws" are needed. The sick, the aged, the blind, the lame, and even the vagrant, has always a house and home, and food and raiment, as far as he considers he needs it. A stranger may, at first sight, think a Samoan one of the poorest of the poor, and yet he may live ten years with that Samoan and not be able to make him understand what *poverty* really is, in the European sense of the word. "How is it?" he will always say. "*No food!* Has he no friends? *No house to live in!* Where *did* he grow? Are there no houses belonging to his friends? Have the people there no love for each other?"

CHAPTER XIV.

CANOES.

Next to a well-built house, Samoan ingenuity was seen in their canoes. Any one could fell a tree, cut off the branches, and hollow out the log some fifteen feet long, for a common fishing canoe in which one or two men can sit. But the more carefully-built canoe, with a number of separate planks raised from a keel, was the work of a distinct and not very numerous class of professed carpenters. The keel was laid in one piece, twenty-five to fifty feet long, as the size of the canoe might be, and to that they added board after board, not by overlapping and nailing, but by *sewing* each close to its fellow, until they had raised it some two, or, it might be, three feet from the ground. These boards were not sawn, squared, and uniform, but were a number of pieces, or *patches*, as they are called, varying in size from eighteen inches to five feet long, as the wood split up from the log with felling axes happens to suit; all, however, were well fastened together, and, with the help of a little gum of the bread-fruit tree for pitch, the whole was perfectly water-tight. In dressing each board, they left a ledge, or rim, all round the edge, which was to be inside, making it double the thickness at the edge to what it was in the middle of the board. It is through this ledge or rim they bored the holes, and with a few turns of cinnet sewed tight one board to the other. The sewing only appeared on the inside. Outside all was smooth and neat; and it was only on close inspection you could see that there was a join at all. They had timbers, thwarts, and gunwale, to keep all tight; and over a few feet at the bow and the stern they had a deck, under which they could stow away anything. The decked part at the bow was the seat of honour, and there you generally saw the chief of the travelling party sitting cross-legged, at his ease, while the others were paddling.

The width of a canoe varied from eighteen to thirty inches; the length, from fifteen to fifty feet. But for an outrigger, it was impossible to keep such a long, narrow thing steady in the water. The outrigger may be described, in any boat, by laying oars across at equal distances, say one right above a thwart. Make fast the handle of each oar to the gunwale on the starboard side of the boat, and let the oars project on the larboard side. To the end of each projecting oar make fast four small sticks running down towards the water, and let their ends also be fastened to a long thick piece of wood, sharp at the one end to cut through the water, and floating on the surface parallel to the boat. This being done will give any one an exact idea of a Polynesian outrigger, by means of which long narrow canoes are kept steady in the water.

Some people who sketch and engrave from imagination, err in representing the natives of Samoa as *pulling* their short paddles, as the European boatman pulls his long oars. The paddle is about four feet long, something like a sharp-pointed shovel; and when the natives paddle, they sit with their faces in the direction in which the canoe is going, "*dig*" in their paddles, send the water flying behind them, and forward the canoe shoots at the rate of seven miles an hour They have always a sail for their canoe, as well as paddles, to take advantage of a fair wind. The sail is triangular, and made of matting. When set, the base is up, and the apex down, quite the reverse of what we see in some other islands. The *mat* sails, however, are giving place to cloth ones, made in the form of European boat-sails.

Some two or three generations back the Samoans built large double canoes like the Fijians. Latterly they seldom built anything larger than a single canoe, with an outrigger, which might carry from fifteen to twenty people. Within the last few years the native carpenters have tried their

127

hand at boat-building, and it is astonishing to see how well they have succeeded in copying the model of an English or American whaleboat, sharp at both ends, or having "two bows," as they call it. Some of them are fifty feet long, and carry well on to one hundred people. From stem to stern there is not a nail; everything is fastened in their ancient style, with cinnet plaited from the fibre of the cocoa-nut husk. Cinnet is likely long to prevail in *native* canoe and boat-building. Although it looks clumsy, it has the advantage of not rotting the wood like an iron nail. It is durable also. With care, and the sewing once or twice renewed, a Samoan canoe or boat will last ten or twenty years.

They did not paint their canoes, but decorated them with rows of white shells (*Cyprœa ovula*) running along the middle of the deck at the bow and stern, and also along the upper part of the outrigger. Now and then they had a figure-head with some rude device of a human figure, a dog, a bird, or something else, which had from time immemorial been the "coat-of-arms" of the particular village or district to which the canoe belonged. A chief of importance must also have one, or perhaps two, large shells in his canoe, to answer the purpose of trumpets, to blow now and then as the canoe passed along. It attracted the attention of the villagers, and called them out to look and inquire, "Who is that?" The ambition to see and to be seen was as common in Polynesia as anywhere else. As the canoe approached any principal settlement, or when it reached its destination, there was a special too-too-too, or flourish of their shell trumpets, to herald its approach. The paddlers at the same time struck up some lively chant, and, as the canoe touched the beach, all was wound up with a united shout, having more of the *yell* in it, but the same in meaning as a "hip, hip, hurrah!"

The French navigator Bougainville, seeing the Samoans so often moving about in their canoes, named the group "The Navigators." A stranger in the distance, judging from the name, may suppose that the Samoans are noted among the Polynesians as enterprising navigators. This is not the case. They are quite a domestic people, and rarely venture out of sight of land. The group, however, is extensive, and gives them some scope for travel. It numbers ten inhabited islands, and stretches east and west about 200 miles. Within these bounds they have kept up an intercourse from the earliest times in their history, which is fully proved, not only by tradition, but by the uniformity of customs and language which prevails from the one end of the group to the other.

CHAPTER XV.

ARTICLES OF MANUFACTURE.

Fishing-nets of various kinds were in use, and were all manufactured on the islands. Several of the Polynesian tribes excel in this branch of industry. A captain of a ship of war, who was buying curiosities lately at Savage Island, actually refused their fine small fishing-nets, thinking that they must be articles of *European* manufacture. In Samoa, net-making is the same now as it was of old. It is the work of the women, and confined principally to the *inland* villages. One would have thought that it would be the reverse, and that the *coast* districts would have made it their principal business. The trade being confined to the interior, is probably occasioned by its proximity to the raw material which abounds in the bush, viz. the bark of the hibiscus, already referred to in describing "fine mats."

After the rough outer surface of the bark has been scraped off with a shell on a board, the remaining fibres are twisted with the mere palm of the hand across the bare thigh into a strong whip-cord, or finer twine, according to the size of the meshes of the net. As the good lady's cord lengthens, she fills her netting-needle, and when that is full, works it into her net. Their wooden netting-needles are exactly the same in form as those in common use in Europe. One evening, in taking a walk, Mrs. Turner and I stood for a few minutes and looked at a woman working a net. Mrs. Turner begged to be allowed to do a bit, took the needle, and did a few loops, to the no small amazement of the woman, who wondered how a European lady could know how to handle a *Samoan* netting-needle, and do *Samoan* work.

They make nets of all sizes, from the small one of eighteen inches square to the seine of a hundred feet long. A net forty feet long and twelve feet deep can be had for native mats, or white calico, to the value of twenty shillings. A hundred men may be able to muster some twenty nets. These they unite together, and, in the lagoon off their settlement, take large quantities of mullet and other fish.

The pearl-shell fish-hook is another article long in use, and in the manufacture of which the Samoans show some ingenuity. They cut a strip off the shell, from two to three inches long, and rub it smooth on a stone, so as to resemble a small fish. On the under side, or what may be called the belly, of this little mock fish, they fasten a hook made of tortoise-shell, or, it may be, nowadays, an English steel one. Alongside of the hook, concealing its point, and in imitation of the fins of a little fish, they fasten two small white feathers. Without any bait, this pearl-shell contrivance is cast adrift at the stern of a canoe, with a line of twenty feet, and from its striking resemblance to a little fish it is soon caught at, and in this way the Samoans secure a large quantity of their favourite food. No European fish-hook has yet superseded this purely native invention. They bait and use the steel fish-hook, however, and in some cases use it on their pearl-shells, as we have just remarked, instead of the tortoise-shell fish-hook.

A curious native drill is seen in connection with the manufacture of these little shell fish-hooks. Fine holes are drilled through the shell for the purpose of making fast the hook as well as the line, and the instrument to which we refer answers the purpose admirably. For the sake of comparison with other parts of the world, this simple contrivance is worth a few lines of description. Take a piece of wood, eighteen inches long, twice the thickness of a cedar pencil. Fasten with a strong thread a fine-pointed nail, or a sail-needle, to the end of this sort of spindle. Get a thick piece of wood, about the size of what is called in England a "hot cross bun," and in Scotland a "cookie," bore a hole in the centre of it, run the spindle through it, and wedge it fast about the middle of the spindle. At the top of the spindle fasten two strings, each nine inches long, to the ends of these strings attach the ends of a common cedar pencil, forming a triangle with a wooden base and string sides. Stand up the machine with your left hand, place the iron point where you wish to bore a hole, and steady the spindle with your left hand. Take hold of the pencil handle of the upper triangle, twirl round the spindle with your left hand, which will coil on the strings at the top to the spindle, pull down the pencil handle quickly, and then the machine will spin round. Work the handle in this way up and down, like a pump, the cord will alternately run off and on to the spindle, and the machine will continue to whirl round, first one way and then the other, until the pearl-shell, or whatever it may be, is perforated.

There is hardly anything else in the department of manufacture requiring particular notice. When speaking of garments, we referred to *native cloth* and *mats*. Large quantities of *cinnet* are plaited by the old men principally. They sit at their ease in their houses, and twist away very rapidly. At political meetings also, where there are hours of formal palaver and speechifying, the old men take their work with them, and improve the time at the cleanly, useful occupation of twisting cinnet. It is a substitute for twine, and useful for many a purpose, and is now sold to the merchants at about a shilling per pound. *Baskets* and *fans* are made as of old of the cocoa-nut leaflet, *floor mats* and a finer kind of baskets from the pandanus leaf. Twenty or thirty pieces of the rib of the cocoa-nut leaflet, fastened close together with a thread of cinnet, form a *comb*. Oval *tubs* are made by hollowing out a block of wood. *Clubs*, three feet long, from the iron-wood, or something else that is heavy. *Spears*, eight feet long, were made from the cocoa-nut tree, and barbed with the sting of the ray-fish; a wicked contrivance, for it was meant to break off from the spear in the body of the unhappy victim. In nine cases out of ten there was no way of cutting it out, and the poor creature died in agony.

The Samoans are an agricultural rather than a manufacturing people. In addition to their own individual wants, their hospitable custom in supplying, without money and without stint, the wants of visitors from all parts of the group, was a great drain on their plantations. The fact that a party of natives could travel from one end of the group to the other without a penny of expense for food and lodging, was an encouragement to pleasure excursions, friendly visits, and all sorts of travelling. Hardly a day passed without there being some strangers in the "guest house" of the village, to be provided for by a contribution from every family in the place. After meeting fully, however, all home wants, large quantities of yams, taro, and bananas, with pigs and poultry, were still to spare, and were sold to the ships which called for water and supplies.

CHAPTER XVI.

GOVERNMENT AND LAWS.

A hurried glance, from a European stand-point, has caused many passing visitors to conclude that the Samoans had nothing whatever in the shape of government or laws. In sailing along the coast of any island of the group, you can hardly discern anything but one uninterrupted mass of bush and vegetation, from the beach to the top of the mountains; but, on landing, and minutely inspecting place after place, you find villages, plantations, roads, and boundary walls, in all directions along the coast. It is the same with their political aspect. It is not until you have landed, lived among the people, and for years closely inspected their movements, that you can form a correct opinion of the exact state of affairs. To any one acquainted with the aborigines of various parts of the world, and especially those of the Papuan groups in Western Polynesia, the simple fact that the Samoans have had but one dialect, and free intercourse with each other all over the group, is proof positive that there must have long existed there *some* system of government.

A good deal of order was maintained by the union of two things, viz. *civil power* and *superstitious fear.*

I. As to the first of these, their government had, and still has, more of the patriarchal and democratic in it, than of the monarchical. Take a village, containing a population, say, of three to five hundred, and there will probably be found there from ten to twenty titled heads of families, and one of the higher rank called chiefs. The titles of the heads of families are not hereditary. The son may succeed to the title which his father had, but it may be given to an uncle, or a cousin, and sometimes the son is passed over, and the title given, by common consent, to a perfect stranger, merely for the sake of drawing him in, to increase the numerical strength of the family. What I now call a family is a combined group of sons, daughters, uncles, cousins, nephews, nieces, etc., and may number fifty individuals. They have one large house, as a common rendezvous, and for the reception of visitors, and four or five other houses, all near each other.

The chiefs, on the other hand, are a most select class, whose pedigree is traced most carefully in the traditionary genealogies to the ancient head of some particular clan. One is chosen to bear the title, but there may be other individuals, who trace their origin to the same stock, call themselves chiefs too, and any of whom may succeed to the title on the death of the one who bears it. A chief, before he dies, may name some one to succeed him, but the final decision rests with the heads of families as to which of the members of the chief family shall have the title and be regarded as the village chief. In some cases the greater part of a village is composed of parties who rank as chiefs, but, as a general rule, it consists of certain families of the more common order, which we have just mentioned, and some titled chief, to whom the village looks up as their political head and protector. It is usual, in the courtesies of common conversation, for all to call each other chiefs. If you listen to the talk of little boys even, you will hear them addressing each other as *chief* this, that, and the other thing. Hence, I have heard a stranger remark, that the difficulty in Samoa is, not to find who is a chief, but to find out who is a common man.

As the chief can call to his aid, in any emergency, other chiefs connected with the same ancient stock from which he has sprung, and as he looks upon the entire village as his children, and feels bound to avenge their wrongs, it is thought essential to have some such head in every settlement. If anything in the clubbing way is to be done, no one but the chief, or his brother, or his son, dare do it. With few exceptions, he moves about, and shares in every-day employments, just like a common man. He goes out with the fishing party, works in his plantation, helps at house-building, and lends a hand at the native oven. There are still, however, although not at first sight to a European eye, well-defined marks of his chieftainship. If you listen to the conversation of the people, or attend a meeting of the heads of families for any village business, you hear that he is addressed with such formalities as might be translated into our English Earl, Duke, Prince, or King So-and-so; and, instead of the plebeian *you*, it is, your Highness, your Grace, your Lordship, or your Majesty. When the ava-bowl is filled, and the cup of friendship sent round, the first cup is handed to him. The turtle, too, the best joint, and anything choice, is sure to be laid before the chief. Then again, if he wishes to marry, the heads of families vie with each other in supplying him with all that is necessary to provide for the feasting, and other things connected with the ceremonies. He, on the other hand, has to give them ample compensation for all this, by distributing among them the fine mats which he gets as the dowry by his bride. A chief is careful to marry only in the family of a chief, and hence he has, by his wife, a portion worthy of the rank of a chief's daughter. To some extent, these heads of families are the *bankers* of the chief. His fine mats almost all go to them, and other property too. They, again, are ready with a supply whenever he wishes to draw upon them, whether for fine mats, food, or other property.

No lover of money was ever fonder of gold than a Samoan was of his fine mats. Hence the more wives the chief wished to have, the better the heads of families liked it, as every marriage was a fresh source of fine mat gain. To such an extent was this carried on, that one match was hardly over before another was in contemplation. If it did not originate with the chief, the heads of families would be concocting something, and marking out the daughter of some one as the object of the next fine mat speculation. The chief would yield to them, have the usual round of ceremonies, but without the remotest idea of living with that person as his wife. In this way a chief, in the course of his lifetime, might be married well on to fifty times; he would not, however, probably have more than two living with him at the same time. As the heads of families were on the look-out to have the *sons* and *daughters* of the chief married as often as they could also, it can be imagined that the main connecting links between the heads of families and their chief, and that which marked him out most prominently as a superior, was this marriage, or rather polygamy business.

The land in Samoa is owned alike by the chiefs and these heads of families. The land belonging to each family is well known, and the person who, for the time being, holds the title of the family head, has the right to dispose of it. It is the same with the chiefs. There are certain tracts of bush or forest land which belong to them. The uncultivated bush is sometimes claimed by those who own the land on its borders. The lagoon also, as far as the reef, is considered the property of those off whose village it is situated. Although the power of selling land, and doing other things of importance affecting all the members of the family, is vested in the titled head of the family, yet the said responsible party dare not do anything without formally consulting all concerned. Were he to persist in attempting to do otherwise, they would take his title from him, and give it to another. The members of a family can thus take the title from their head, and heads of families can unite and take the title from their chief, and give it to his brother, or uncle, or some other member of the chief family, who, they think, will act more in accordance with their wishes.

The chief of the village and the heads of families formed the legislative body of the place, and the common court of appeal in all cases of difficulty. One of these heads of families was the sort of Prime Minister of the chief. It was his special business to call a meeting, and it was also his province to send notice to the other heads of families, on the arrival of a party of strangers, and to say what each was to provide towards entertaining hospitably the village guests. Having no written language, of course they had no written laws; still, as far back as we can trace, they had well understood laws for the prevention of theft, adultery, assault, and murder, together with many other minor things, such as disrespectful language to a chief, calling him a pig, for instance, rude behaviour to strangers, pulling down a fence, or maliciously cutting a fruit-tree. Nor had they only the mere laws; the further back we go in their history, we find that their penalties were all the more severe. Death was the usual punishment for murder and adultery; and, as the injured party was at liberty to seek revenge on the brother, son, or any member of the family to which the guilty party belonged, these crimes were all the more dreaded and rare. In a case of murder, the culprit, and all belonging to him, fled to some other village of the district, or perhaps to another district; in either case it was a city of refuge. While they remained away, it was seldom any one dared to pursue them, and risk hostilities with the village which protected them. They might hear, however, that their houses had been burned, their plantations and land taken from them, and they themselves prohibited, by the united voice of the chief and heads of families, from ever again returning to the place. Fines of large quantities of food, which provided a feast for the entire village, were common; but there were frequently cases in which it was considered right to make the punishment fall exclusively on the culprit himself. For adultery, the eyes were sometimes taken out or the nose and ears *bitten* off. I was called into a house one day to doctor the *nose* of a young dame who had just suffered from the incisors of a jealous woman. A story is told of a husband and wife who made up their minds to end their jealousies by a separation. When all was ready, and the woman was about to leave the house with her share of the mat and other property, she said to the man: "Now, let us again salute noses and part in peace." The simpleton yielded, but instead of the friendly touch and *smell*, the vixen fastened on to the poor fellow's *gnomon*, and disfigured him for life.

For other crimes they had some such punishments as tying the hands of the culprit behind his back, and marching him along naked, something like the ancient French law of "amende honorable;" or, tying him hand to hand and foot to foot, and then carrying him suspended from a prickly pole run through between the tied hands and feet, and laying him down before the family or village against whom he had transgressed, as if he were a *pig* to be killed and cooked; compelling the culprit to sit naked for hours in the broiling sun; to be hung up by the heels; or to beat the head with stones till the face was covered with blood; or to play at handball with the prickly sea-urchin; or to take five bites of a pungent root, which was like filling the mouth five times with cayenne pepper. It was considered cowardly to shrink from the punishment on which the village court might decide, and so the young man would go boldly forward, sit down before the chiefs, bite the root five times, get up and walk away with his mouth on fire.

If two families in a village quarrelled, and wished to fight, the other heads of families and the chief stepped in and forbad; and it was at the peril of either party to carry on the strife contrary to the decided voice of public opinion.

These village communities, of from two to five hundred people, considered themselves perfectly distinct from each other, quite independent, and at liberty to act as they pleased on their own ground, and in their own affairs.

Then, again, these villages, in numbers of eight or ten, united by common consent, and formed a district, or state, for mutual protection. Some particular village was known as the capital of the district; and it was common to have a higher chief than any of the rest, as the head of that village, and who bore the title of King. Just as in the individual villages the chief and heads of families united in suppressing strife when two parties quarrelled, so it was in the event of a disturbance between any two villages of the district, the combined chiefs and heads of families of all the other villages united in forbidding strife. When war was threatened by another district, no single village acted alone; the whole district, or state, assembled at their capital, and had a special parliament to deliberate as to what should be done.

These meetings were held out of doors. The heads of families were the orators and members of parliament. The kings and chiefs rarely spoke. The representatives of each village had their known places, where they sat, under the shade of bread-fruit trees, and formed groups all round the margin of an open space, called the malæ (or forum), a thousand feet in circumference. Strangers from all parts might attend; and on some occasions there were two thousand people and upwards at these parliamentary gatherings. The speaker stood up when he addressed the assembly, laid over his shoulder his fly-flapper, or badge of office similar to what is seen on some ancient Egyptian standards. He held before him a staff six feet long, and leaned forward on it as he went on with his speech. A Samoan orator did not let his voice fall, but rather gradually raised it, so that the last word in a sentence was the loudest. It is the province of the head village to have the opening or king's speech, and to keep order in the meeting; and it was the particular province of another to reply to it, and so they went on. To a stranger the etiquette and delay connected with such meetings was tiresome in the extreme. When the first speaker rose, other heads of families belonging to his village, to the number of ten or twenty, rose up, too, as if they all wished to speak. This was to show to the assembly that the heads of families were all at their post, and who they were. They talked among themselves for a while, and it ended in one after another sitting down, after having passed on his right to speak to another. It was quite well known, in most cases, who was to speak, but they must have this preliminary formality about it. At last, after an hour or more all had sat down but the one who was to speak; and, laden by them with the responsibility of speaking, he commenced. He was not contented with a mere *word* of salutation, such as, "Gentlemen," but he must, with great minuteness, go over the names and titles, and a host of ancestral references, of which they were proud. Another half-hour was spent with this. Up to this time conversation went on freely all round the meeting; but whenever he came to the point of his address, viz., the object of the meeting and an opinion on it, all was attention. After the first speech, it was probably mid-day, and then food was brought in. The young men and women of the family, decked off in their best, came in a string of ten or twenty to their chief, each carrying something, and, naming him, said it was food for him. He told them to take it to So-and-so, and then they marched off to that chief, and said that it was food from such a one. This person would return the compliment by-and-by, and in this way there was, for hours, a delightful flow of friendship all over the place. On such occasions parties who had been living at variance had a fine opportunity of showing kindness to each other. Amid all this feasting the speechifying went on. As the debate advanced, the interest increased. They generally broke up at sundown; but if it was something of unusual interest and urgency, they went on speechifying in the dark, or in the moonlight, and might not adjourn till long after midnight. Unless all were pretty much agreed, nothing was done. They were afraid to thwart even a small minority.

Throughout the Samoan group there were, in all, *ten* of these separate districts such as I have described. In war some of the districts remained neutral, and of those engaged in the strife there might be two against one, or three against five, or, as in a late prolonged war, five against two. The district which was conquered, was exposed to the taunts and overbearing of their conquerors. But a subdued district seldom remained many years with the brand of "conquered." They were up and at it as soon as they had a favourable opportunity, and were probably themselves in turn the conquerors.

II. But I hasten to notice *the second thing* which I have already remarked was an auxiliary towards the maintenance of peace and order in Samoa, viz. *superstitious fear*. If the chief and heads of families, in their court of inquiry into any case of stealing, or other concealed matter, had a difficulty in finding out the culprit, they would make all involved swear that they were innocent. In swearing before the chiefs the suspected parties laid a handful of grass on the stone, or whatever it was, which was supposed to be the representative of the village god, and, laying their hand on it, would say, "In the presence of our chiefs now assembled, I lay my hand on the stone. If I stole the thing may I speedily die." This was a common mode of swearing. The meaning of the grass was a silent additional imprecation that his family might all die, and that *grass* might grow over their habitation. If all swore, and the culprit was still undiscovered, the chiefs then wound up the affair by committing the case to the village god, and solemnly invoking him to mark out for speedy destruction the guilty mischief-maker.

But, instead of appealing to the chiefs, and calling for an oath, many were contented with their own individual schemes and imprecations to frighten thieves and prevent stealing. When a man went to his plantation and saw that some cocoa-nuts, or a bunch of bananas, had been stolen, he would stand and shout at the top of his voice two or three times, "May fire blast the eyes of the person who has stolen my bananas! May fire burn down his eyes and the eyes of his god too!" This rang throughout the adjacent plantations, and made the thief tremble. They dreaded such uttered imprecations. Others cursed more privately when a thing was stolen, and called in the aid of a priest. In common disputes also, affecting the veracity of each other, it was customary for the one to say to the other, "Touch your eyes, if what you say is true." If he touched his eyes, the dispute was settled. It was as if he had said, "May I be cursed with blindness if it is not true what I say." Or the doubter would say to his opponent, "Who will eat you? Say the name of your god." He whose word was doubted would then name the household god of his family, as much as to say, "May god So-and-so destroy me, if what I have said is not true." Or the person whose word was doubted might adopt the more expressive course still of taking a stick and digging a hole in the ground, which was as if he said, "May I be buried immediately if what I say is not true." But there was another and more extensive class of curses, which were also feared, and formed a powerful check on stealing, especially from plantations and fruit-trees, viz. the silent hieroglyphic taboo, or tapui (tapooe), as they call it. Of this there was a great variety, and the following are specimens:—

1. *The sea-pike taboo.*—If a man wished that a sea-pike might run into the body of the person who attempted to steal, say, his bread-fruits, he would plait some cocoa-nut leaflets in the form of a sea-pike, and suspend it from one or more of the trees which he wished to protect. Any ordinary thief would be terrified to touch a tree from which this was suspended, he would expect that the next time he went to the sea, a fish of the said description would dart up and mortally wound him.

2. *The white shark taboo* was another object of terror to a thief. This was done by plaiting a cocoa-nut leaf in the form of a shark, adding fins, etc., and this they suspended from the tree. It was tantamount to an expressed imprecation, that the thief might be devoured by the white shark the next time he went to fish.

3. *The cross-stick taboo.*—This was a piece of any sort of stick suspended horizontally from the tree. It expressed the wish of the owner of the tree, that any thief touching it might have a disease running right across his body, and remaining fixed there till he died.

4. *The ulcer taboo.*—This was made by burying in the ground some pieces of clam-shell, and erecting at the spot three or four reeds, tied together at the top in a bunch like the head of a man. This was to express the wish and prayer of the owner that any thief might be laid down with ulcerous sores all over his body. If a thief transgressed, and had any subsequent swellings or sores, he confessed, sent a present to the owner of the land, and he, in return, sent back some native herb, as a medicine, and a pledge of forgiveness.

5. *The tic-doloureux taboo.*—This was done by fixing a spear in the ground close by the trees which the owner wished to guard. It was expressive of a wish that the thief might suffer from the face and head agonies of the disease just named.

6. *The death taboo.*—This was made by pouring some oil into a small calabash, and burying it near the tree. The spot was marked by a

little hillock of white sand. The sight of one of these places was also effectual in scaring away a thief.

7. *The rat taboo.*—This was a small cocoa-nut leaf basket, filled with ashes from the cooking-house, and two or three small stones, and suspended from the tree. It signified a wish that rats might eat holes in the fine mats of the thief, and destroy any cloth, or other property which he might value.

8. *The thunder taboo.*—If a man wished that lightning might strike any who should steal from his land, he would plait some cocoa-nut leaflets in the form of a small square mat, and suspend it from a tree, with the addition of some white streamers of native cloth flying. A thief believed that if he trespassed he, or some of his children, might be struck with lightning, or, perhaps his own trees struck and blasted from the same cause. They were not, however, in the habit of talking about the effects of *lightning*. It was the *thunder* they thought did the mischief; hence they called that to which I have just referred, the *thunder* taboo.

From these few illustrations it will be observed that Samoa formed no exception to the remarkably widespread system of superstitious taboo; and the extent to which it preserved honesty and order among a heathen people will be readily imagined. At the present day the belief in the power of these rude hieroglyphics is not yet eradicated. In passing along you still see something with streamers flying, dangling from a tree in one place, a basket suspended in another, and some reeds erect in a third. The sickness, too, and dying hours of some hardened thief still bring out confessions of his guilt. Facts such as these which have just been enumerated still further show the cruelties of the reign of superstition, and exhibit, in striking contrast, the better spirit and the purer precepts taught by that blessed volume which is now received, read, and practised by many in Samoa. In days of heathenism there was no good rendered for evil there, and the only prayers for injurers and enemies were curses for their hurt and destruction.

CHAPTER XVII.

WARS.

The murder of a chief, a disputed title, or a desire on the part of one, two, or more of the districts, to be considered stronger and of more importance than the rest, were frequent causes of war in Samoa. Hostilities were often prevented by such acts as giving up the culprit, paying a heavy fine, or by bowing down in abject submission, carrying firewood and small stones used in baking a pig, or, perhaps, a few bamboos. The firewood, stones, and leaves, were equivalent to their saying, "Here we are, your pigs, to be cooked if you please; and here are the materials with which to do it." Taking bamboos in the hand was as if they said, "We have come, and here are the knives to cut us up." A piece of split bamboo was, of old, the usual knife in Samoa. If, however, the chiefs of the district were determined to resist, they prepared accordingly. The boundary which separated one district from another was the usual battlefield; hence the villages next to that spot, on either side, were occupied at once by the troops. The women and children, the sick and the aged, were cleared off to some fortified place in the bush, or removed to some other district which was either neutral, or could be depended upon as an ally. Movable property was either buried, or taken off with the women and children. The wives of the chiefs and principal men generally followed their husbands wherever they might be encamped, to be ready to nurse them if sick or wounded. A heroine would even follow close upon the heels of her husband in actual conflict, carrying his club or some other part of his armour.

It was common for chiefs to take with them a present of fine mats when they went to another district to solicit help in war, but there was no standing army or regularly paid soldiers anywhere. When the chiefs decided on war, every man and boy under their jurisdiction old enough to handle a club had to take his place as a soldier, or risk the loss of his lands and property, and banishment from the place.

In each district there was a certain village, or cluster of villages, known as "the advance troops." It was their province to take the lead, and in battle their loss was double the number of that of any other village. Still they boasted of their right to lead, would on no account give it up to others, and talked in the current strain of other parts of the world about the "glory" of dying in battle. In a time of peace the people of these villages had special marks of respect shown to them, such as the largest share of food at public feasts, flattery for their bravery, etc.

While war was going on the chiefs and heads of families united in some central spot, and whatever they decided on, either for attack or defence, the young men endeavoured implicitly to carry out. Their weapons were clubs, spears, and slings. Subsequently, as iron was introduced, they got hatchets, and with these they made their most deadly weapon, viz. a sharp tomahawk, with a handle the length of a walking-stick. After that again they had the *civilised* additions of swords, pistols, guns, and bayonets. Around the village where the war party assembled they threw a rough stockade, formed by any kind of sticks or trees cut into eight feet lengths, and put close to each other, upright, with their ends buried two feet in the ground. The hostile parties might be each fortified in this way not more than a mile from each other, and now and then venture out to fight in the intervening space, or to take each other by surprise at weak or unguarded points. In their war canoes they had some distinguishing badge of their district hoisted on a pole, a bird it might be, or a dog, or a bunch of leaves. And, for the bush-ranging land forces, they had certain marks on the body by which they knew their own party, and which served as a temporary watchword. One day the distinguishing mark might be blackened cheeks; the next, two strokes on the breast; the next, a white shell suspended from a strip of white cloth round the neck, and so on. Before any formal fight, they had a day of feasting, reviewing, and merriment. In action they never stood up in orderly ranks to rush at each other. According to their notions that would be the height of folly. Their favourite tactics were rather of the surprise and bush-skirmishing order. In some of their fights in recent times I have known of from two to fifty killed on each side in a battle, never more. Prisoners, if men, were generally killed; if women, distributed among the conquerors. In a battle which was fought in 1830 a fire was kindled and many of the prisoners were burned.

Their heroes were the swift of foot, like Achilles or Asahel; men who could dash forward towards a crowd, hurl a spear with deadly precision, and stand for a while tilting off with his club other spears as they approached him within an inch of running him through. They were ambitious also to signalise themselves by the number of *heads* they could lay before the chiefs. No hero at the Grecian games rejoiced more over his chaplet than did the Samoan glory in the distinction of having cut off a man's head. As he went along with it through the villages on the way to the place where the chiefs were assembled, awaiting the hourly news of the battle, he danced, and capered, and shouted, calling out every now and then the name of the village, and adding, "I am So-and-so, I have got the head of such an one." When he reached the spot where the chiefs were met, he went through a few more evolutions, and then laid down the head before them. This, together with the formal thanks of the chiefs before the multitude for his bravery and successful fighting, was the very height of a young man's ambition. He made some giddy, frolicsome turns on his heel, and was off again to try and get another victim. These heads were piled up in a heap in the malae or public assembly. The head of the most important chief was put on the top, and, as the tale of the battle was told, they would say, "There were so many heads, surmounted by the head of So-and-so," giving the number and the name. After remaining for some hours piled up they were either claimed by their relatives or buried on the spot. A rare illustration of this ambition to get heads occurred about thirty years ago. In an unexpected attack upon a village one morning a young man fell stunned by a blow. Presently he recovered consciousness, felt the weight of some one sitting on his shoulders and covering his neck, and the first sounds he heard was a dispute going on between two as to which of them had the right to cut off his head! He made a desperate effort, jostled the fellow off his back, sprang to his feet, and, with his head all safe in his own possession, soon settled the matter by leaving them both far behind him.

The headless bodies of the slain, scattered about in the bush after a battle, if known, were buried, if unknown, left to the dogs. In some cases the whole body was pulled along in savage triumph and laid before the chiefs. One day, when some of us were in a war-fort endeavouring to mediate for peace, a dead body of one of the enemy was dragged in, preceded by a fellow making all sorts of fiendish gestures, with one of the legs in his teeth cut off by the knee.

Connected with Samoan warfare several other things may be noted, such as consulting the gods, taking a priest to battle to pray for his people and curse the enemy, filling up wells, destroying fruit-trees, going to battle decked off in their most valuable clothing and trinkets, haranguing each other previous to a fight, the very counterpart of Abijah the king of Judah, and even word for word, with the filthy-tongued Rabshakeh.

If the war became general, and involving several districts, they formed themselves into a threefold division of highway, bush, and sea-fighters. The fleet might consist of three hundred men, in thirty or forty canoes. The bushrangers and the fleet were principally dreaded, as there was no calculating where they were, or when they might pounce unawares upon some unguarded settlement. The fleet met apart from the land forces, and concocted their own schemes. They would have it all arranged, for instance, and a dead secret, to be off after dark to attack a particular village belonging to the enemy. At midnight they would land at an uninhabited place some miles from the settlement they intended to attack. They took a circuitous course in the bush, surrounded the village from behind, having previously arranged to let the canoes slip on quietly, and take up their position in the water in front of the village. By break of day they rushed into the houses of the unsuspecting people before they had well woke up, chopped off as many heads as they could, rushed with them to their canoes, and decamped before the young men of the place had time to muster or arm. Often they were scared by the people, who, during war, kept a watch, night and day, at all the principal openings in the reef; but now and then the plot succeeded and there was fearful slaughter. It was in one of these early morning attacks from the fleet that the young man to whom I have referred had such a narrow escape. That morning many were wounded, and the heads of thirteen carried off. One of them was that of a poor old man, who was on his knees at his morning devotions, when off went his head at a blow. In another house that same morning there was a noble instance of maternal heroism, in a woman who allowed herself to be hacked from head to foot, bending over her son to save his life. It is considered cowardly to kill a woman, or they would have despatched her at once. It was the head of her little boy they wanted, but they did not get it. The poor woman was in a dreadful state, but, to the surprise of all, recovered.

It is now close upon a hundred years since the Samoans had their first serious quarrel with Europeans, and which ended in a fight. I refer to the massacre at Tutuila of M. de Langle and others belonging to the expedition under the unfortunate La Perouse in 1787, and which branded the people for well-nigh fifty years as a race of treacherous savages whose shores ought not to be approached. Had the native version of the tale been known, it would have considerably modified the accounts which were published in the voyages of La Perouse. The origin of the quarrel was not with the party who went on shore in the boats. A native who was out at the ship was roughly dealt with, for some real or supposed case of pilfering. He was fired at and mortally wounded, and when taken on shore bleeding and dying, his enraged friends roused all on the spot to seek instant revenge. Hence the deadly attack on the party in the boats at the beach, in which the stones flew like bullets and ended in the death of M. de Langle, his brother officer, and ten of the crew. The natives wound up the bodies of the Frenchmen in native cloth and decently buried them, as they were in the habit of burying their own dead. The only inference which ought to have been drawn from this tragic occurrence was that heathen natives have a keen sense of justice, and that if men will go on the disproportionate principle of a life for a tooth, and shoot a man for a perfect trifle, they must abide by the consequences. It is almost certain to be avenged, and, alas! it is often the case that vengeance falls not on the guilty, but on some unsuspecting visitor who may subsequently follow.

CHAPTER XVIII.

THE HEAVENS,
AND THE HEAVENLY BODIES.

1. The Samoans say that of old the *heavens fell down*, and that people had to crawl about like the lower animals. After a time the arrow-root and another similar plant pushed up the heavens, and the place where these plants grew is still pointed out and called the Teengâlangi, or heaven-pushing place; but the heads of the people continued to knock on the skies, and the place was excessively hot. One day a woman was passing along who had been drawing water. A man came up to her and said he would push up the heavens if she would give him some water to drink. "Push them up first," she replied. He pushed them up, and said, "Will that do?" "No," said she, "a little farther." He sent them up higher still, and then she handed him her cocoa-nut shell water-bottle. Another account says that the giant god Ti'iti'i pushed up the heavens, and that at the place where he stood there are hollow places in a rock nearly six feet long which are pointed out as his footprints.

2. Tradition says that in former times the people on earth had frequent *intercourse with the heavens*. We have already noticed some of these visits (pp. 13, 105). These stories are probably founded on the old idea that the heavens ended at the horizon. They thought that there was solidity there as well as extension; and therefore a distant voyage to some other island might be called a visit to some part of the heavens.

When white men made their appearance, it was thought that they and the vessel which brought them had in some way broken through the heavens; and, to this day white men are called Papalangi, or Heaven-bursters.

But imagination required something more circumstantial, and hence the variety of traditionary schemes by which the people were supposed to go up and down on these visits to the heavens. One story speaks of a mountain, the top of which reached to the skies. Another says that a very dense column of smoke took people up. Another tells of a tree which, when it fell, was sixty miles in length. Another tree is mentioned which formed a sort of ladder, but on different sections of it there were repulsive or stinging insects, through which few but the very courageous persevered in forcing their way. First there was a part swarming with cockroaches; then a place full of ants; then a section covered with large venomous ants; beyond that again was a part of the tree overspread with centipedes, from which many turned and went down again to *terra firma*. The centipede region cleared, however, some finer branches were reached, and perched on them, the tourists waited for a high wind, which swung them up and down for a time, and then they were suddenly jerked in to the heavens.

3.   Some curious stories are told about *the sun*. A woman called Mangamangai became pregnant by looking at the rising sun. Her son grew and was named "Child of the Sun." At his marriage he applied to his mother for a dowry. She sent him to his father, the sun, to beg from him, and told him how to go. Following her directions he went one morning with a long vine from the bush—which is the convenient substitute for a rope—climbed a tree, threw his rope with a noose at the end of it, and caught the sun. He made known his message, and (Pandora-like) got a present for his bride. The sun first asked him what was his choice—blessings or calamities? "Blessings,"

was his reply, and he came down with a store of them done up in a basket. There is another tale told about this Samoan Phaethon similar to what is related of the Hawaiian Maui. He and his mother were annoyed at the rapidity of the sun's course in those days—it rose, reached the meridian, and set, "before they could get their mats aired." He determined to make it go slower. He climbed a tree in the early morning, and with a rope and noose threw again and caught the sun as it emerged from the horizon. The sun struggled to get clear, but in vain. Then fearing lest he should be strangled he called out: "Have mercy on me—spare my life—what do you want?" "We wish you to go slower," was the reply, "we can get no work done." "Very well, let me go; for the future I will walk slowly." He let go the rope, and ever since the sun has gone slowly and given longer days.

The sun was the usual *timekeeper* of the day. The night was divided into three parts—midnight, and the first and second cock-crowing. Then came the sun. There was the rising—the half-way up—the standing straight overhead—turning over—making to go down—and, last of all, sinking. They thought the blazing sun went down into the ocean, passed through and came up next morning on the other side. The commotion among the waves at the horizon as he went down was supposed to be very great, and it was one of the worst curses to wish a person to sink in the ocean and the sun to go blazing down on the top of him.

Human sacrifices to the sun are spoken of in some of the more remote traditions. In this connection Papatea in the Eastward again comes up as the place where the sacrifices were offered. When the sun rose he called for a victim, and the same when he set. This continued for eighty days, and the population of the island was fast passing away. A lady called Ui, and her brother Luamaa, fled from Papatea and reached Manu'a, but alas! the sun there too was demanding his daily victims. It went the round of the houses, and when all had given up one of their number it was again the turn of the first house to supply an offering. The body was laid out on a Pandanus tree, and there the sun devoured it. It came to the turn of Luamaa to be offered, but his sister Ui compassionated him, and insisted on being offered in his stead. She lay down and called out: "Oh, cruel Sun! come and eat your victim, we are all being devoured by you." The sun looked at lady Ui, desired to live with her, and so he put an end to the sacrifices, and took her to wife. Another story makes out that Ui was the daughter of the King of Manu'a, and that he gave up his daughter as an offering to the sun, and so end the sacrifices by making her the saviour of the people.

4. Some of *the planets* are known and named. Fetŭ is the word used to designate all heavenly bodies except the sun and moon. Venus is called the morning and evening star. Mars is the Matamemea, or the star with the sear-leafed face. The Pleiades are called Lii or Mataalii, eyes of chiefs. The belt of Orion is the amonga, or burden carried on a pole across the shoulders. The milky way is ao lele, ao to'a, and the aniva. Ao lele, means flying cloud, and ao to'a, solid cloud. Meteors are called, fetŭ ati afi, or stars going to fetch a light; and comets are called pusa loa, or an elongated smoke.

5. Tradition in Samoa, as in other parts of the world, has a good deal to say about *the moon*. We are told of the visit to it by two young men, the one named Punifanga and the other Tafaliu. The one went up by a tree, and the other on a column of dense smoke from a fire kindled by himself for the purpose. We are also told of the woman Sina, or *white*, who with her child has long been up there. She was busy one evening with mallet in hand beating out on a board some of the bark of the paper mulberry with which to make native cloth. It was during a time of famine. The moon was just rising, and reminded her of a great bread-fruit, looking up to it she said, "Why cannot you come down and let my child have a bit of you?" The moon was indignant at the thought of being eaten, came down forthwith, and took her up, child, board, mallet, and all. At the full of the moon

young Samoa still looks up, and traces the features of Sina, the face of the child, and the board and mallet, in verification of the old story.

The moon was *the timekeeper of the year*. The year was divided into twelve lunar months, and each month was known by a name in common use all over the group. To this there were some local exceptions, and a month named after the god, who on that month was specially worshipped. It is said that of old it was universal to name the month after the god whose worship at that particular time was observed. Among a people who had no fixed astronomical dates intercallation was easy, and the names of the twelve moons kept uniform.

January.

1. This was called Utu va mua, *first yam digging*. And so named from their then digging wild yams before the cultivated ones were ripe, and also from early yam digging.
2. Others say that the origin of Utu va mua was in two brothers, the one called Utuvamua and the other Utuvamuli, who, when there was war in heaven, and their party beaten, fled to the earth and brought the January storms with them.
3. A third account says that Utuvamua was the elder brother and Utuvamuli the younger, and that during a great war on earth they escaped to the heavens. That the hills are the heaps of slain covered over by earth dug up from the valleys, and that when the two brothers look down upon them their weeping and wailing and maddening exasperation occasion the storm and the hurricane.
4. The month was also called Aitu tele, *great god*, from the principal worship of the month. At another place it was named Tangaloa tele, for a similar reason.

February.

1. This month was called Toe utu va, or *digging again*, and so named from the yam crop.
2. The name is also explained as the further digging up of the winds to raise storms.
3. Aitu iti, or *small gods*, is another name, from the worship of the inferior household gods in that month.

March.

1. Called Faaafu, or *withering*, from the withering of the yam vine and other plants, which become coloured "like the shells."
2. Taafanua is another name of the month, which means, *roam* or *walk about the land*, being the name of a god worshipped in that month.
3. Called also Aitu iti, or small gods, from the household gods then worshipped, and who were specially implored to bless the family for the year "with strength to overcome in quarrels and in battle."

April.

1. This month was called Lo, from the name of a small fish which comes in plentiful shoals at that time.
2. Called also Fanonga, or *destruction*, the name of a god worshipped at the eastern extremity of the group during that month.

May.

1. Called Aununu, or *stem crushed*, from the crushed or pulverised state of the stem of the yam at that time. Others say it was so named from multitudes of malicious demons supposed to be wandering about at that time. Even the fish of the sea were supposed to be possessed and unusually savage in this month. May is often an unhealthy month,

being the time of transition from the wet season to the dry, and hence the *crushing* sickness and superstitious vagaries.

2. Called also on one island Sina, or *white*, from the worship of a goddess of that name there.

June.

This month was called Oloamanu, or *the singing of birds*, it was thus named from the unusual joy among the birds over a plentiful supply of favourite buds and berries. The bright scarlet flowers of the "*Erythrina indica*" begin then to come out and attract a host of parrakeets and other happy chirpers.

July.

Called Palolo mua, or *the first of Palolo*. This is the first month of the half year, called the Palolo season in contradistinction to the other half, which is called the Trade-wind season. Palolo (*Palolo virides*) is that singular worm which swarms out from certain parts of the barrier reefs for three days in the course of a year, of which the natives are very fond, and all the more so from its rareness. If the last quarter of the moon is late in October palolo is found the day before, the day of, and the day after, that quarter. If the last quarter of the moon is early in October palolo does not come till the last quarter of the November moon. The middle day, or the day of the quarter, is the principal day for gathering these swarms of marine worms.

August.

This month was called Palolo muli, or *after Palolo*. Pa means to burst, and lolo, fatty or oily, and hence probably the origin of the name in the fatty or oily appearance of the worms as they break, burst, and are mixed up in the heaps directly after they are taken. They are only found for about half an hour before sunrise, after sunrise they disappear.

September.

1. Mulifâ was the name given to this month which means *end of the stem* of the talo, or "arum esculentum." The month being unusually dry and parching, the scorching rays of the sun left little of the talo stem but a small piece at the end.
2. The *end* of the season for catching the fish called Fâ, is another derivation of Mulifâ given by some.

October.

This month was called Lotuaga, or *rain prayers*. It was so called from the special prayers which were then offered to the gods for rain.

November.

Taumafamua was the name of this month, *the first of plenty*, that means, fish and other food became plentiful, and then followed what were called the palolo and fly-hook feasts. Public dinners in the houses of the leading men of the village were the order of the day.

December.

This month was named Toetaumafa, or *the finish of the feasting*. Food now was less plentiful, and after some of the December gales or cyclones there was a great scarcity.

CHAPTER XIX.

THE ORIGIN OF FIRE, AND OTHER STORIES.

1. The Samoans say that there was a time when their ancestors ate everything raw, and that they owe the luxury of cooked food to one Ti'iti'i, the son of a person called Talanga. This Talanga was high in favour with the earthquake god Mafuie, who lived in a subterranean region where there was fire continually burning. On going to a certain perpendicular rock, and saying, "Rock, divide! I am Talanga; I have come to work!" the rock opened, and let Talanga in; and he went below to his plantation in the land of this god Mafuie. One day Ti'iti'i, the son of Talanga, followed his father, and watched where he entered. The youth, after a time, went up to the rock, and, feigning his father's voice, said, "Rock, divide! I am Talanga; I have come to work!" and was admitted too. His father, who was at work in his plantation, was surprised to see his son there, and begged him not to talk loud, lest the god Mafuie should hear him, and be angry.

Seeing smoke rising, he inquired of his father what it was. His father said it was the fire of Mafuie. "I must go and get some," said the son. "No," said the father; "he will be angry. Don't you know he eats people?" "What do I care for him?" said the daring youth; and off he went, humming a song, towards the smoking furnace.

"Who are you?" said Mafuie.

"I am Ti'iti'i, the son of Talanga. I am come for some fire."

"Take it," said Mafuie.

He went back to his father with some cinders, and the two set to work to bake some taro. They kindled a fire, and were preparing the taro to put on the hot stones, when suddenly the god Mafuie blew up the oven, scattered the stones all about, and put out the fire. "Now," said Talanga, "did not I tell you Mafuie would be angry?" Ti'iti'i went off in a rage to Mafuie, and without any ceremony commenced with, "Why have you broken up our oven, and put out our fire?" Mafuie was indignant at such a tone and language, rushed at him, and there they wrestled with each other. Ti'iti'i got hold of the right arm of Mafuie, grasped it with both hands, and gave it such a wrench that it broke off. He then seized the other arm, and was going to twist it off next when Mafuie declared himself beaten, and implored Ti'iti'i to have mercy, and spare his left arm.

"Do let me have this arm," said he; "I need it to hold Samoa straight and level. Give it to me, and I will let you have my hundred wives."

"No, not for that," said Ti'iti'i.

"Well, then, will you take *fire*? If you let me have my left arm you shall have *fire*, and you may ever after this eat cooked food."

"Agreed," said Ti'iti'i; "you keep your arm, and I have *fire*."

"Go," said Mafuie; "you will find the fire in every *wood* you cut."

And hence, the story adds, Samoa, ever since the days of Ti'iti'i, has eaten cooked food from the fire which is got from the friction of rubbing one piece of dry *wood* against another.

The superstitious still have half an idea that Mafuie is down below Samoa somewhere; and that the earth has a long handle there, like a walking-stick, which Mafuie gives a shake now and then. It was common for them to say, when they felt the shock of an earthquake, "Thanks to Ti'iti'i, that Mafuie has only one arm: if he had two, what a shake he would give!"

The natives of Savage Island, 300 miles to the south of Samoa, have a somewhat similar tale about the origin of fire. Instead of Talanga and

Ti'iti'i, they give the names of Maui, the father, and Maui, the son. Instead of going through a rock, their entrance was down through a reed bush. And, instead of a *stipulation* for the fire, they say that the youth Maui, like another Prometheus, *stole* it, ran up the passage, and before his father could catch him, he had set the bush in flames in all directions. The father tried to put it out, but in vain; and they further add, that ever since the exploit of young Maui, they have had *fire* and cooked food in Savage Island.

2. The Samoans have their stories of *a golden age* of intelligence long long ago, when *all* things material had the power of speech. They not only spoke, but they had evil natures as well, and quarrelled with each other and fought, very much like the races of mankind. We have already referred to the early battles of cosmogony, and to the wars of the rocks and fires and earth and stones. It was the same with the flora and fauna. Or to give it in their own words: "The small stones fought with the grass, the stones were beaten and the grass conquered. The short grass fought with the strong weedy grass, the short grass was beaten and the strong grass conquered. The strong grass fought with the long grass of the bush, the strong grass was beaten and the bush grass conquered. The bush grass fought with the trees, the grass was beaten and the trees conquered. The trees fought with the creepers, the trees were beaten and the creepers conquered—and then began the wars of men." Pity but the wars of *men* had been as bloodless as those which preceded them!

The principle seems to be that whenever one thing prevails to excess above another thing, or is in any way superior, be it rock, stone, earth, grass, or tree, we are sure to find some tradition of its battle and victory. The old poetic Samoan forefathers who framed these fabulous fights added a deal of circumstance and minuteness to their tales, and all was seriously believed by some of their more prosaic posterity.

3.   A story is told of *a battle between two trees*—a Fijian Banian tree and the Samoan tree called Tatangia (*acacia laurifolia*). A report reached Samoa that the trees of Fiji had fought with the Banian tree, and that it had beaten them all. On this the Tatangia and another tree went off from Samoa in two canoes to fight the Fijian champion. They reached Fiji, went on shore, and there stood the Banian tree. "Where is the tree," they inquired, "which has conquered all the trees?" "I am the tree," said the Banian. Then said the Tatangia, "I have come to fight with you." "Very good, let us fight" replied the Banian. They fought. A branch of the Banian tree fell, but Tatangia sprung aside and escaped. Another fell—ditto, ditto—the Tatangia. Then the trunk fell. Tatangia again darted aside and escaped unhurt. On this the Banian tree "buried its eyes in the earth," and owned itself conquered. As many of the towns and districts are spoken of figuratively by the names of trees noted for strength or beauty, the inference as to the real actors in these tree fights is obvious. The present generation, however, will hardly admit that they may describe the wars of *men*.

The following is a specimen story of a piscatorial fight:—A shark which had its habitat in a cave on the south side of Savaii mustered all the fish in the neighbourhood to go and fight with the great red fish of Manu'a. The Manu'a fish with their red leader met them in the ocean between Tutuila and Manu'a. They fought. The Savaii fish were beaten, and fled pursued by their conquerors. Most of them took refuge under stones and rocks and escaped, but their leader, the shark, fled to his own cave. He was pursued, however, and killed by the red fish of Manu'a. I tell them that the shark, red fish, etc., must have been mere figurative names for chiefs and districts, and the finny troops under them were doubtless living *men*, but in all these stories the Samoans are rigid literalists, and believe in the very words of the tradition. And yet at the present day they have towns and districts bearing figurative names, distinct from the real names, such as the sword fish, the stinging ray, the dog, the wild boar, the Tongan cock, the frigate bird, etc. And if such creatures had been known of old in Samoa, they would no doubt have had their bear, their lion, and their eagle, and stories too of their battles.

4. We have also accounts of battles fought by the birds on the one side and the fish on the other. The fish and the birds were in the habit of paying friendly visits to each other. The inanga, or small fry of a fresh-water fish, were offended at not being hospitably received on shore by the birds; on the other hand, the birds despised the inanga for being so small. They fought, and the fishes conquered, and it ended in the fish becoming birds and the birds fishes; and hence they say the back-bone of the inanga projects so much. But after that there was another battle, in which the fish were beaten and the birds conquered; and ever since the birds have had their wings, and their supremacy, and the right of going to the sea, or the river, as they please, to pick up the fish which come within their reach.

A battle also between the owl and the serpent is noteworthy. It runs as follows:—There were ten brothers, whose names were Sefulu, Iva, Valu, Fitu, Ono, Lima, Fa, Tolu, Lua, and Tasi, and so named from the ten numerals, which in those days began with Sefulu as 1, and ended with Tasi as 10. These ten brothers went to the forest to cut wood for a large canoe. They came upon an owl and a serpent fighting. Sefulu was walking first, and to him the owl called out; "Sefulu, you come and kill my enemy here, the serpent, and if you do, you shall have a right to the Ifilele and Maota timber trees" [*Afzelia bijuga*, and *Dysoxylon Sp.*]

"No, let us pass on," said Sefulu, "there are plenty of other trees which will answer our purpose." Then the owl turned to Iva and all the others on to Lua, and implored help in killing the serpent, but each in turn answered as did Sefulu. Tasi, however, replied to the entreaty of the owl, and said, "Yes, I will," and grasping his felling axe, struck out at the serpent and killed it. "Well done, Tasi!" said the owl, "and to keep in remembrance for all time to come your bravery, and respect for me, you shall stand foremost in everything that is numbered. Sefulu who has been *first* shall now be *last*, and you who have been last shall always be first." And so it has continued to the present day—the first, Tasi, and the tenth, Sefulu.

5.   The appearance or forms of things, as in this latter instance perhaps, have also suggested some other *fabulous stories*. They say that the rat had wings formerly, and that the large bat or flying fox at that time had no wings. One day the bat said to the rat: "Let me try on your wings for a little, that I may see how I like flying." The rat lent the bat his wings, off flew the bat with the wings, and never came back to return them. And hence the proverb applied to a person who borrows and does not return: "Like the bat with the rat."

Take another illustration. With the exception of the mountain plantain (*Musa uranospatha*) all the bananas have their bunches of fruit hanging downwards towards the earth, like a bunch of grapes.

The plantain shoots up its bunch of fruit erect towards the heavens. As the reason of this, we are told that of old all the bananas held their heads erect, but they quarrelled with the plantain, fought, were beaten, and, ever since, have hung their heads in token of their defeat, whereas the plantain is erect still, and the symbol of its own victory.

6.   They have a number of *other fabulous stories* referred to in proverbial language in daily use. Take the story of the fowl and the turtle. A fowl made her headquarters over a rock from which a cool spring of fresh water ran out into the adjacent stream. One day a turtle made its appearance. It was enjoying the cool fresh bath, and rising now and then to look about, when it was addressed roughly by the fowl: "Who are you?" "I am a turtle." "Where have you come from?"

"From the hot salt sea." "What are you doing here?" "Bathing, and enjoying the fine cool fresh water." "Be off, this is my water." "No, it is mine as much as it is yours." "No, it is mine, and you must be off." "No I won't. I have as much right to be here as you." "Well, then," said the fowl, "let us decide in this way which of us will have it. Let each of us go away, and whoever is *first* here in the morning shall have the right to the spring." "Let it be so," said the turtle, "I'm off to the briny sea; you go away to the village."

The turtle was back from the sea, up the river, and at the spring, very early in the morning. The fowl thought there was no need to hurry, as she could with *one* bound on her wings be at the rock; and so she roosted till the sun was rising, and then flew over to the rock, but there was the turtle before her! "You are there, I see," said the fowl. "Yes, I am," replied the turtle, "and the spring is mine." And hence the proverb applied to the lazy and the late: "Here comes the fowl, the turtle is before you!"

7. Here is another of these fabulous stories:—There were three friends, a rat, a snipe, and a crab. They thought they would like to look about them on the sea, and so decided to build a canoe and go out on a short cruise. They did so, and when the canoe was ready off they went. The snipe pulled the first paddle, the crab the second, and the rat steered. A squall came on, and the canoe upset. The snipe flew to the shore, the crab sank and escaped to the bottom, and the rat swam. The rat was soon fatigued, but an octopus came along, and from it the rat implored help. "Come on my back," said the octopus. The rat was only too happy to do so. By-and-by the octopus said: "How heavy you are! my back is getting painful." "Yes," said the rat, "I drank too much salt water when I was swimming there; but bear it a little longer, we shall soon be at the shore."

When the octopus reached the shore off ran the rat into the bush. The octopus felt the pain still, however, and now discovered that the rat had been gnawing at the back of its neck. The octopus was enraged, called all his friends among the owls to assemble, and begged them to pursue and destroy the rat. They did so, caught it, killed it, and ate it, but there was hardly a morsel for each, they were so many. And hence the proverb in exhorting not to return evil for good:—"Do not be like the rat with the octopus, evil will overtake you if you do."

8. Here is a story of Toa and Pale, or Hero and Helper.

The King of Fiji was a savage cannibal, and the people were melting away under him. Toa and Pale were brothers, they wished to escape being killed for the oven, and so fled to the bush and became trees. It was only the day before a party were to go to the woods to search for a straight tree from which to make the keel of a new canoe for the king. They knew this, and so Pale changed himself into a crooked stick overrun with creepers, that he might not be cut by the king's carpenters, and advised Toa to do the same. He declined, however, and preferred standing erect as a handsome straight tree.

The party in search of a keel went to the very place, liked the look of Toa, and decided to cut it down. They cut, and Toa was felled to the ground, but Pale, who was close by, immediately raised him up again. The carpenters were confounded—cut again—but it was just the same. They persevered, and the cutting, falling, and rising again, went on till night fell, when they gave it up. After they left Toa said to Pale, "What a Toa (trouble) I have been to you!" and hence *the proverb* to this day, when a person or thing has been a trouble to another, he says to the sufferer in a sympathising or apologetic tone: "*What a Toa it has been to you!*"

9. The following are a few more of these *proverbs*, but stated more briefly.

(1) "One and yet a thousand," is a common description of a clever man, and equivalent to our own expression: "He is a host in himself."

(2) "Only the appearance of plait." Spoken of a thin worn-out person reduced to a mere shadow. Not a real plaited mat, but only the appearance of one.

(3) "Many footprints." Spoken of a large settlement which makes many at a festival, or night-dance, or public meeting of any kind.

(4) "A single cocoa-nut." Referring to a single nut hanging from a tree. This is said of a man who has no brothers, and who is therefore called the single nut of the family.

(5) "Great and yet small." Applied to a populous place which has no *courage*. Or a large family, but without one who has any pluck.

(6) "The emptiness of a large basket." A good deal of food seems but little if put in a large basket. Also the population of a large village, if the houses are widely apart, seems small until they really come together.

(7) "The break of a cocoa-nut leaf net." This leaf net is an arrangement for enclosing fish by a long string of cocoa-nut leaves, which, if the leaves break, can be easily tied again. This is spoken of a chief who dies but leaves a number of sons to take his place.

(8) "Afterwards touched." If a family is numerically strong, no one dares to injure them. If, however, a number die, then those who survive are more liable to insult or injury from the neighbourhood. In the event of such ill-usage they throw it back on their injurers: "You dared not touch us before."

(9) "Helping with the burden." As one may run in and stretch out his hand to ease the shoulder of a weak person struggling under a load, so a person who prompts a public speaker in a difficulty is said to help with the burden.

(10) "Covering the dead bird." If a pigeon sees its mate fall dead it will drop down and cover the body with its wings even if it should be killed also. To this the Samoans compare a brother who will rush in among troops after his wounded brother even if he should be killed himself.

CHAPTER XX

NAMES OF THE ISLANDS.

Illustrating Migrations, etc.

1. Of the group generally, it is said that a couple lived at Pulotu called Head of Day and Tail of Day. They had four children—(1) Ua, or *Rain*; (2) Fan, *Long grass*;(3) Langi, *Heavens*; (and 4) Tala, or *Story*. The four went to visit Papatea. Pulotu is in the west, Papatea in the east. The Papateans heard of the arrival of the four brothers and determined to kill them. First, Ua was struck on the neck; and hence the word *taua*, or beat the neck, as the word for war. This was the beginning of wars. Others stood on the neck of Fan, and hence the proverb in war: "To-morrow we shall tread on the neck of Fan." Others surrounded and spat on Langi, and hence the proverb for ill-usage, or rudely passing before chiefs: "It is spitting on Langi." Tala was spared, and escaped uninjured.

Tala and Langi returned to Pulotu and told about their ill-usage. Then Elo, the king of Pulotu, was enraged, and prepared to go and fight the Papateans. This was the first war in history. They went, they fought, they conquered, and made a clean sweep of Papatea; and hence the proverb: "Like the rage of Elo." Also for a village destroyed in battle they say: "Ua faa Papateaina"—*made to be like Papatea.*

All who fled to the bush were sought and killed, only those who fled to sea escaped. A man called Tutu and his wife Ila reached the island of Tutuila, and named it so by the union of their names. U and Polu reached Upolu, and hence the name of that island by uniting their names. Sa and Vaila reached Savaii, united their names also, and, for the sake of euphony, or, as they call euphony "lifting it easily," made it Savaii instead of Savaila.

Elo and his warriors went back to Pulotu. Langi and Tala after a time came to Samoa, but went round by way of Papatea,[3] and from them also the people of Manono and Apolima are said to have sprung.

2   MANU'A.—This name embraces three islands at the east end of the Samoan group. Manu'a means *wounded*. As the story runs, the rocks and the earth married, and had a child, which, when born, was covered with *wounds*; and hence the name of the said small group of three islands.

The story of Lu figures here again. He had a son who was named Moa, after his preserve fowls, and this Moa became king of Manu'a. From that time fowls were no longer called *Moa* on Manu'a, but Manu lele, or *winged creatures*, out of respect to the name of the king.

Fitiaumua, or *Fiji the foremost*, is also mixed up with Manu'a history. He was said to have come from the east, was a great warrior, conquered at Fiji, and in his lust for conquest came to Samoa. He subdued all the leeward islands of the group, reached Manu'a, and there he dwelt. All Samoa took tribute to him, and hence the place was called the Great Manu'a.

(1.)   *Taŭ* is the name of the principal island of Manu'a. Its principal village is also called Taŭ. It is said to have had its name from the child of Faleile-langi—*House roofed by the heavens*, that is to say, no house at all, and alluding to the remote tradition of a time when people had no houses. This lady was the daughter of the god Tangaloa, and had a child who was *dumb*, and from that child she named the island Taū. Ū expresses the hollow unintelligible sound emitted by the dumb.

Fitiuta, or Inland Fiji, is the name of a principal village. It was formerly called Anga'e, or *Breathing hard*, from the hard breathing at its birth of a child of Rocks and Earth. But the name was changed. Moiuuoleapai, a daughter of Tangaloa, married the king of Fiji and went and lived there. She was ill-used and sent to the backwoods of Fiji. Taeotangaloa heard that his sister was being ill-treated, and went off to Fiji to see if it was true. It was true. He stood by her, cheered her solitude, and by a great yam and banana plantation he turned the bush into a fruitful garden. The king of Fiji heard of it, went and made up matters with his cast-off wife, as he much wished the yams, which were scarce at the time, and hence the proverb: "Do you call them friends who are but friendly to the *yam?*" The king named the fertile spot Fitiuta, and when Taeotangaloa returned to Manu'a he changed the name of the village from Anga'e to Fitiuta.

(2.)   *Olosenga* is the central island in the Manu'a group. This was called the land of the god Fuailangi, *Originator of the heavens*. He dug up the earth on the land of the chief Niuleamoa on Taū. The latter pushed it off into the sea as a floating island, jumped on to it with the god Fuailangi, together with a lady called Olo, and other two chiefs named Puletainuu and Masuitufanga. Away they went to Tonga, seeking some place suitable for the residence of a war god. They returned to Samoa, touched at Savaii and Upolu, and then went to Tutuila, but as the people there began to make a dunghill of their floating island, they went back to Manu'a, and rested between Taū and Ofu, as Fuailangi thought he could there fight at pleasure with the people on either side of him.

Senga, the chief of Ofu, looked out, was surprised to see the new island, went over to look at it, and soon after married Lady Olo. They united their names, and called it *Olosenga*. The god Fuailangi in after years was in repute, and dreaded. He was incarnate in the sea eel, had an altar which the people carried about with them, and any persons cooking or eating the sea eel had their eyes burned and their scalps clubbed as a punishment. Another story is that some parrots flew ashore from a Fiji canoe. Olo means *fort* and Senga a *parrot*, and hence the island was called Olosenga—the fort or refuge of parrots.

(3.)   *Ofu* is the name of a third island at Manu'a. Ofu means *clothed*. Faleile-langi, the daughter of Tangaloa, had another child, and this one they clothed, and, in remembrance of the early tailoring, the island was called Ofu.

3.   TUTUILA.—The prevailing story of the origin of the name of this island is the one already referred to. Tutu the man and Ila the woman came from the eastward, and dwelt on the island. They had a daughter born to them there and called her Salaia. When weak and dying they begged that after their death their names might be remembered.

After they passed away Salaia, or, as some call her, Sangaia, united the names of her parents, and named the island Tutuila.

4.   NUUTELE is a small island off the east end of Upolu. It is said to have been so named from two men who came to seek a steersman for the king of Fiji. Nuu was the name of the one, and Tele the other. The union of their names became the name of the island.

5.   UPOLU.—There are a number of diverse stories as to the origin of this name, as is the case with all these ancient legends.

(1.) The most prevailing fragment is the one already alluded to of the two called U and Polu who fled from Papatea. Their united names became the name of the island. They had a son, and they named him king of Upolu. He called his village the Malae, or meeting-place of Upolu, and all the gods of the group assembled there at times. It was here they met to discuss the question as to the duration of human life (see p. 9).

(2.) Upolu was said to be the capital of Pulotu. In a time of war a number of people fled from Pulotu, reached this island of the Samoan group, and called it Upolu, in remembrance of their native land.

(3.) Timuateatea, *Wide-spreading rain*, the daughter of Tangaloa of the heavens, married a chief on earth called Beginning. They had a son called Polu. The father, in thinking of some employment for his boy, looked over to the mountains of Savaii, and it occurred to him that it would be well to get a canoe and go over and see whether there were people over there or only mountains. He called Polu, and told him to go up to his grandfather in the heavens and fetch some carpenters, that they might build a canoe, cross the channel and explore Savaii. Polu refused, but at length yielded and went up. The carpenters did not care about the job, but Polu was most urgent, and would take no denial. U is the word for *urge*. His grandfather asked the name of his island. Polu said it had none; and on this Tangaloa said: "Very well, when you go down call it Upolu, in remembrance of your being so urgent on the carpenters."

6. MANONO, a small island, 3 miles in circumference, between Upolu and Savaii, has the following historic fragments:—

(1.) Nono came from Fiji. He was the son of Tuiolautala, king of Fiji. There came with him Sa'umâ, the brother of the king, and

Tupuivao, the god of Fiji. A family quarrel about a fish led them to come away. Their canoe made the land between Savaii and Upolu. The god Tangaloa came down and stood on the bow of their canoe and told them not to go to Savaii or Upolu, lest they should be trampled upon, but remain where they were. Then Tupuivao vomited a quantity of land he had swallowed at Fiji, and so made Manono and its neighbouring island Apolima. He also appointed Sa'umâ to live on the latter, and Nono to take up his abode on Manono, which they so named from Mâ and Nono.

(2.) The chief Lautala came from Fiji on a war expedition. He first touched at Manu'a, and then came and conquered Upolu. After that he lived on Manono. He made a net, fished, and hung it up to dry. In the night a number of gods came and tore it to pieces. Lautala then attacked the gods, and drove them off with great slaughter. He could not count the number killed, but supposed them to be *Mano*, or ten thousand, and hence the name of the island Manono.

(3.) Lautala was the name of an island at Fiji, and noted for war. It broke away from Fiji, and was brought sailing along the ocean to Samoa by the chief Nono, who came to seek a suitable place for carrying on war. He first went to Manu'a, but did not like it. He then went to the space between Tutuila and Upolu, but did not fancy that either. Then he came to the space between Upolu and Savaii, and thought that would do, as he could attack Upolu or Savaii, whichever he pleased. He anchored his island there, where it now is, and named it Manono, after himself. Hence it is said that Manono is not a part of Samoa, but a fragment of Fiji, and that of old there was no land between Upolu and Savaii.

7. APOLIMA is a small island three miles from Manono. Manono and Apolima were two sons of the king of Fiji. One day Manono cooked an oven of yams for his father and brother chiefs, but served it up without a fish. His father was angry, and so off went Manono with a spear and speared a fish and took it to his father. His father was still angry, and hurled a spear at him. He fell, pulled it out of his neck, and got up and ran off to Samoa.

Apolima remained still in Fiji, but after a time came in search of his brother and found him where he now is. Before he left Fiji his father told him to call himself Apo-i-le-lima, or Apolima, which means, *Poised in the hand*, from the spear which he held when he speared Manono. They have been often attacked, but never conquered, from their impregnable island fortress. It is a great high hollow basin-shaped island, inaccessible all round but at one narrow chip in the west side of the basin, which can be easily defended.

8. SAVAII is the largest island of the group, and the name is accounted for in various ways:—

    (1.)   The king who propped up the heavens had a wife called Flying Clouds, and two children, the one was called Savaii the Great, and the other Upolu the Great. Savaii dwelt on Savaii, and Upolu on Upolu, and gave their names to their respective islands.

    (2.)   A couple came from Fiji, the one was named Sa and the other Vaii, or Vaiki, according to some. They landed at the south-west side of the island, and lived there. Vaii, the husband, died, and then Sa put her name first and united the two, as Savaii, the name of the island.

    (3.)   Two brothers, the one called Vaii, and the other Polu, with their sister, Vavau, came from the east. The young woman, Vavau, divided the land—told Polu to go to Upolu, and Vaii to remain on Savaii. Her name is perpetuated in the word, which as a noun, means "ancient times," and, as an adjective, is used to express ancient, perpetual, and everlasting.

FOOTNOTES:

3   There is an island called Maatea in the Paumotu group.

CHAPTER XXI.

POLITICAL DIVISIONS AND PLACES OF NOTE ON UPOLU.

On Upolu the name of Pili has an early place among the doings of mortals and in the division of the lands. In one of the traditions his history runs thus:—Manga had a daughter called Sina, who married the king of Manu'a. They had a daughter called Sinaleana, *White of the cave*, because she lived in a cave in which there was also kept the parrot of the king. The god, Tangaloa, of the heavens looked down and fancied her. He sent Thunder and Storm for her; they did not get her. Lightning and Darkness were also sent to fetch her, but they also failed. Next Deluging Rain, dashing down in great egg-drops, was sent, but to no purpose. He then let down a net, which covered up the mouth of the cave, caught her, and pulled her up to the heavens. She became his wife, had a child, and named him Pili, or *Entangled*, from the way in which she was entangled in the net.

Pili grew up to manhood under the care of the gods, and was sometimes told, pointing down to the earth, that that place was his. He begged of his father Tangaloa to be allowed to go down. The reply was: "If you go down, come up again. But if you wish to go and not return, take my wooden pillow and fishing-net with you."

He was let down to the earth by the fishing-net, and placed on Manu'a. The king of Manu'a asked where he came from, and on hearing that he was his grandson, and that his mother, Sina, was still up in the heavens, he wept aloud. Pili went to visit Tutuila, tried his hand at fishing, but caught nothing, and was mocked by the Tutuilans. He then swam away to Savaii, took up his abode at the village Aopo, and from that was called Piliopo. He quarrelled with the chief there and went off to the village called Palapala, where he met with Tavaetele, *Great tropic bird*, who had come from Aana on Upolu to seek taro plants. The Palapala people were generous, and presented the Upolu chief with 100,000 plants. The retinue of the chief made a difficulty about taking so many across the channel, but Pili stepped forward and said he would bring them all over himself, which he actually did, and helped in making a taro plantation, which extended from the one side of Aana to the other, right across the island. He remained there and married Sina, the daughter of this chief.

Pili and his wife had four children. First there were twins, the one called Tua and the other Ana. Tua was so named from the *back* of a turtle which Pili caught at that time, and Ana from the *cave* in which it was taken. The next born was called Tuamasanga, or, *After the twins*. Then followed Tolufale, or *Three houses*, from the three houses into which the mother was taken before the child was born.

When Pili was old and dying he called his children together and appointed them their places and employments. To Tua, the eldest, he gave the plantation dibble, as the business of agriculture, and the eastern division of Upolu now called Atua. To Tuamasanga he committed the orator's staff and fly-flapper, with which to do the business of speaking, and, as a residence, the central division of Upolu called Tuamasanga: hence the name of the district there called Sangana, *sacred to oratory*. To Ana he gave the Spear as the emblem of war, and as a district, the western division of Upolu called Aana. Tolufale was to live on Manono, but to go about and take the oversight of all. The old man finished up his will with: "When you wish to fight, fight; when you wish to work, work; when you wish to talk, talk." After his death they separated, and went to their respective places and employments.

1.   ATUA is the eastern division of Upolu, and it again was subdivided into what they called the head, the middle, and the tail.

(1.)   *Aleipata* is a district at the east end of the island, and was called the head, as the titled king or *head* of Atua resided there. The name originated in Alei and Pata, a couple who were said to have come from the heavens and taught their children to build houses. They were very good-looking, and charged their children that when they died they were to be buried in a standing posture, with their faces uncovered, that people might still come and look at them; and from this probably originated the custom of embalming practised there.

Lefao was the name a chief who came from Tutuila and lived in one of the districts bordering on Aleipata. When the meeting was held for the division of the lands of Atua he did not attend, but the chiefs voted him the place and neighbourhood where he lived at Lepa, or the *wall*, which, of old, ran across the island and ended there, and hence the place was named Salefao—sacred to, or, *the province of Lefao.*

(2.)   *Lufilufi.*—This settlement, on the north side, was the principal residence of the kings of Atua. The word means *food-divider.* It had its origin in the name of a fish called Naiufi, which was cut up, on one occasion, with surprising dexterity by one of the king's attendants with only a bit of the cocoa-nut stem as a knife. He received on that account the name of *Lufilufi*, and was promoted to be chief carver to the king, and to rule in all divisions of food on public occasions. The town was named after him, and to this day in all public gatherings the distribution of the food part of the entertainment is committed to some of the young men of this place.

(3.) *Saluafata.*—This village is closely attached to Lufilufi, and was so named from a lady called Luafata who lived there, and whose daughter married the king of Atua. Her grandchild by this royal father was among the indulged, and, like other scions of royalty in Samoa, had such privileges as to stand or walk about when he ate his food; and, while others carried burdens of cocoanuts, etc., he was allowed to march up and down with a fancy spear, and play at spear throwing. He was named the Right-arm-of-Atua, and took the lead in the village as body-guard of the king.

(4.) *Solosolo* means *falling*, and the town was so named from a loose stone wall which the first settlers there built, but which repeatedly fell down. Aumua and Oloatua are the names of two divisions of the settlement, separated by the wall. These were the names of two attendants of a lady called Manu, who had several Samoan suitors but rejected them all, and went to Tonga. Two Tongan kings made proposals to her. The one was good-looking, and the other was more noted for good living and even cannibal preferences. Her attendants advised her to marry the latter, but to try and get her share of the cannibal feast *alive*, and save them. She took their advice, married the gourmand king, and when baked human bodies were laid before her, begged that, for the future, *such* offerings might be presented alive. This was granted, and one after another of her share in the victims was passed over, alive as she got them, to the care of her attendants, Aumua and Oloatua, at a place on the opposite side of the road. By-and-by it became a large village of the saved.

Queen Manu had a daughter called Vaetoeifanga who grew up to womanhood. She was heard of in Samoa, and a lady was sent to Tonga to try and get her to come and marry the king of Aana. The lady described his land as a perfect paradise, with nine springs of water, and she was persuaded to go and be the wife of the king of Aana. When she came to Samoa a number of the people from the village of the saved, with Aumua and Oloatua, came with her, and gave the names to these places at Solosolo. Some of them also went further east and occupied and named some of the settlements about Fangaloa, or the *Long-bay*, as it is called from its running far inland.

Solosolo was also noted as the residence of the cannibal *god*, Maniloa, as he was called. He lived in a valley, and the people worshipped him. As they went with their offerings of food they had to cross a ravine, walking, Blondin style, on a thick vine which the god stretched across the valley. He sat himself in the middle of the said vine-rope, shook it as any one he fancied approached, and down fell the victim dead into the ravine, and ready for the next meal.

A young man called Polu-leuligana, *Polu-of-dark-speech*, son of Malietoa, called one day when on a journey. The people related to him their grievances, and how they were being all eaten up by Maniloa. This daring youth concocted a scheme. He told them to fix upon some one to sit concealed with an axe at the end of the rope next to the village, and that he would go round, axe in hand also, by a circuitous course, and conceal himself close by the end of the rope on the other side of the ravine; there he would watch till the god was again in his place on the centre of the rope, rise up, shout at the top of his voice, and this was to be the signal to cut the rope at each end and let fall their cannibal enemy. They did so. Next day Maniloa went along and sat down on the rope to wait for his victim. Presently the valley rang with a shout, the rope was cut at both ends, and down, crash into the ravine, went the horrid old creature, and ever after Solosolo was saved from his cannibalism.

(5.) *Falealili*, or the House-of-Lili, is the name of a district on the south side of Atua. Lili was a chief from Fiji whose mother was a Samoan. He and some others were driven away from Fiji on

181

account of bad conduct. When he came to Samoa the land had been divided, but he got his share, as *the tail of Atua*. He built a large house, and from this house of Lili the district was named. It embraces a number of villages and adjacent places, named after local circumstances or events. *Salani* was so called from the white coral pebbles on the beach with which the women decorate the graves of the dead. *Salesatele* was also called the *sweat* of Falealili, from the heroism of the people of that place in battle. If the king of Atua was on a journey, and carried along shoulder high, as soon as he reached this village he had to get down and walk, as a mark of respect to the chivalrous villagers. *Faleulu*, or Housed-by-the-bread-fruit-tree, was so named from a party who came from Fiji by way of Manu'a and Tutuila, and who, on reaching Upolu, were benighted there and slept under a bread-fruit tree. The name of *Poutasi*, or One-post, had its origin in a great O'a tree (*Bischoffia javanica*) which a chief ordered to be dug up root and all, planted in the village, and made the centre post of his house. *Lotofanga* is said to have been named after Loto and Fanga, who were sent by the king of Fiji to search for a runaway son. A lagoon is said to have been there once, but was dried up by these first inhabitants of the place pouring hot water into it.

2. TUAMASANGA is the central division of Upolu, having about sixteen miles of coast on the north side, and twelve on the south.

(1.) At *Malie*, in the district of Sangana on the north side, the chief Malietoa had his principal residence when on Upolu; and of the doings there of some of these Malietoas, or "Pleasing-heroes," as the name means, many stories are told. After Polu-leuligana had seen the old cannibal god dead in the ravine at Solosolo (p. 238) he returned to Sangana. On his arrival the first thing he heard was the wailing of a poor lad who had just been brought over from Savaii and was about to be killed for Malietoa's next meal. Polu told him to be quiet, and promised to try and save his life. He ordered the usual green cocoa-nut leaves to be plaited, and *himself* to be done up in them, slung on a pole, carried by two men, and laid down before his father as if it were the baked victim from Savaii. Malietoa saw a bright eye peering through the leaflets, opened, and behold! there was his son Polu-leuligana. He was so touched with this extraordinary condescension of his son that he not only saved the lad who was about to be killed, but further, to mark the day and the event, he declared that from that time no more *human* victims were to be killed for the oven, and that *pigs* were to be used instead. After this Polu was named Faaifoaso, or "Downfall-of-Cannibalism."

Another story is told of the said Malietoa. He was annoyed at the disappearance of some of his bread-fruits, bananas, and fowls, and summoned to Sangana all the priests of the Tuamasanga. Twenty of them assembled. He told them what had been stolen, and ordered them to divine the thief. After a long silence they said they could not tell. They were then tied hand and foot, carried outside, and laid down in the blazing sun till they could declare the name of the thief. At the same time Malietoa sent off to Savaii for a noted conjurer called Vaapuu or "Short-canoe." After some days he arrived, and found the priests still tied up in the sun. On hearing the case he turned to Malietoa and said: "Listen while I tell you the names of the thieves. *The owl* has taken your fowls. *The bat* has eaten your bread-fruits. And the *Kingfisher* bird has made away with your bananas." This was enough. The twenty priests were liberated, went to their respective homes, and told how they owed their lives to the ready reply of the expert Vaapuu.

(2.) *Faleata*, or the "House-of-Ata," embraces a number of small villages, and was so named from the chief Ata. Ata was killed in battle, and his brother Too took it so much to heart that he went away inland, scooped out a great hollow, and filled it with his tears; and hence the lake there called *Lanutoo*, or "Lake-of-Too."

The Faleata people were and still are distinguished for their heroism and clever scheming in war. In a battle on Savaii they fled before the Safune people, or rather *pretended* to flee. While some fled others lay down among the slain as if motionless and dead; and when the Safune people came to search for those of their own who had fallen, up started the living Faleata people with their clubs, rushed at them, and again conquered Safune. Hence a *sham* retreat in war is to this day called "a *Faleata* flight."

(3.) *Apia* is the name of the principal harbour in the Tuamasanga. The word is abbreviated from Apitia, or *straightened*, and the place was so named in remembrance of a battle, in which the Tuamasanga came suddenly down from the bush on to the fleet of Manono canoes, threw them into disorder, and, in their haste to escape, ran upon one another in the narrow passage out of the harbour. The village inland of Apia, called Tanumamanono, or "The-burial-place-of-Manono," keeps up in its name the remembrance of the slain of Manono buried there.

(4.) *Laulii* is the name of a village in the east end of the Tuamasanga. A couple lived there called Lau and Lii, with a party who came from Fiji and took up their abode in the bay there which was called "Sacred to the gods." A large canoe was being built by three chiefs there in the bush. Lau and Lii wished to see it, as it was a very superior one, and to be called, "The canoe without a leak." They mistook the road, wandered, could not

184

find either the canoe or its builders, and were so angry over the disappointment that they changed themselves into two rocks which stand there, and in remembrance of them the place is called Laulii.

(5.) *Laloata* is the name of a village inland of Apia. The word means "Under the shade," and had its origin as follows:—Pai and his wife lived there, and had a daughter called Sina. The woman went down to the sea one day to fetch salt water for cooking purposes; a small sea eel stuck to her cocoa-nut shell water-bottle, and she took it home as a plaything for her child Sina to feed and keep in a cup. The eel grew, and then they digged a well for it. One day Pai and his wife returned from some plantation work and found Sina crying, as the eel had bitten her. They concluded that it must have become the incarnation of some cruel god, and determined to go away from the place.

Away the three went eastward, but on looking round there was the eel out of the water and following after them. Then said the father to his wife and Sina: "You make your escape, and I will remain here and raise mountains to keep it back." Sina and her mother went on ahead, but on looking over their shoulder there was the eel again still rustling after them. Then the mother said to her daughter: "You make your escape alone, and I will remain here, raise mountains and intercept the creature." Sina went on alone, but the eel still followed just as before. As she passed through the villages the people called her in to rest and have a bit of food, and once and again she offered to do so on condition that they would try and deliver her from the pursuing eel. When they heard that, and saw the creature, they said:

"Oh no, you had better pass on; we are afraid of that thing."

Sina gave it up, thought escape was impossible, turned round and made for her home again. As she passed through one of the villages to the east of Apia the people called the attention of their chief to the young woman passing, and an eel following her. He told them to call her in and have something to drink. She said she would gladly do so if they would only get rid of the eel. The chief called out to her: "Yes, come in, and we can do that." She went into the house, and the eel remained outside. The chief gave orders to get ready a cup of 'ava for the strangers, and quietly whispered to the young men to go off to the bush and bring all the poisonous things they could lay their hands on to mix with it. Soon the bowl was brought in, and the 'ava declared ready to be served round.

"Give the first cup to the stranger outside," said the chief to the young men; and out went one of them with a cup to the eel, which was at once eagerly drank. But immediately the creature called to Sina to go outside, and when Sina went out it said to her: "Sina, I am dying. Let us part in peace. When you hear that they have cooked me, you ask the head as your share. Then take it and bury it near the stone wall, and it will grow up a cocoa-nut tree for you. In the nuts you will see my eyes and mouth, and so we shall be able to look at each other face to face still. The leaves of the tree will be a shade for you, and you can plait them into mats, and make a fan also to fan yourself."

After saying this the creature died. It was soon in the oven; and when served up by-and-by Sina begged the head, took it home with her, and put it under the ground near the stone wall. It grew up to be a cocoa-nut tree, and she got her leaves, and mats, and fans, and nuts, marked with the eyes and mouth of her departed eel, which she could kiss still; and there too she had a shade also when she sat down to work or rest—and hence the origin alike of the name of the village, Laloata, and of the introduction of cocoa-nuts.

(6.) *Safata* is the name of the south side of the Tuamasanga. It is said to have had its origin in Sa, who came from Fonaui in Fiji, and Fata of Sangana. Fata had a quarrel with his brother over the Malietoa title, and so determined to leave the family and take up his residence on the other side of the island, and there he met with his friend from Fiji. It contains a number of villages, and a beautiful salt water lagoon connected with the sea by a narrow entrance.

This circular basin is said to have been formed by the dying struggles of a great fish. This "great fish" had its habitat in the straits, and was long the dread of persons crossing the channel between Savaii and Upolu. At length a Savaii man plotted the destruction of the monster. He split up some bamboos, made small knives of them, and tied them together. He also cooked food for the journey, and went off in a canoe with his two sons to search for the fish. He found it, or rather the fish found him, and as it rushed at him with open jaws he called to the boys to crouch down lest they should be injured by the great teeth. Away they went, canoe and all, down the throat of the monster. He then untied his bamboo knives and said: "Now, lads, let us cut away here right and left." It is said in one of the stories that he found some other Samoans there: some were dead, but to others who were still alive he handed a knife each, and said that they too must help in the work of destruction.

"The great fish" was in agony, flew through the ocean towards Upolu, went round the west end, along the south side, rushed in towards the land at Safata, tore up a passage for itself, madly wheeled round and round, and there and then died. The natives there looked on in amazement, and when all was still went down to see what the great carcase was. An enormous prize, and soon they commenced to cut into it with their stone axes. Presently they were startled by a voice from the inside calling out "Strike gently up there!" And who are you? "I am Alo of Palauli; we have been killing this great enemy of ours." He and his sons were soon let out of their prison. Ever after he was called *I'aulualo*, or the "Fish-enterer," and praised for his heroic deed. Some fragments of black rock on one side of the lagoon are said to be the petrified bones of the great sea monster.

3.   AANA is the most westerly division of Upolu.

(1.)   *Alofi Aana,* or the "Gathering of Aana," is the general name of the north side of Aana, and was so called from the gathering of the clans there for club exercise and other sports.

(2.)   *Leulumoenga,* or "Headquarters," is the name of the capital town, and the residence of the king of Aana when they had one. Once upon a time when a king was wanted and they were rather scarce, two daring fellows went to a village thirty miles off, and stole an infant of rank and made him king. They cut their hair short, disguised themselves as *women,* and went to the house in the night when they heard the shout of joy over the birth of the young chief. One of them offered to nurse the baby for a little, and got it. The two slipped out with the child, and off they went in the dark. There was some stir in the house attending to the mother, and when all were settled down some wonder was expressed that the baby was so quiet "Who has it?" went round the house, but, to the amazement of everybody, no one *there* could reply and say "I have." It was days before they found out that while they were thus talking, the child and its captors were far on their way back to Leulumoenga with their prize. They kept him too, and the little man lived to be king of Aana.

(3.)   *Fasitoouta* and *Fasitootai* are two large villages on either side of Leulumoenga. These places trace their origin to Tapuaau, *Swimming-Tapu,* or, as some call him, Tooaau, which means *Swimming-stick.* He is said to have swam from Fiji on a to'oto'o, or walking-stick. He landed at Leulumoenga, married there, and had two sons. When they grew up he divided the wonderful stick, gave one piece or *fasi,* to the one son, and the other *fasi* to the other. The one went to the settlement nearest to the sea westward from Leulumoenga, and called it Fasitootai, or

"Bit-of-the-stick-seaward." The other went farther away and eastward, and called his village Fasitoouta, "Bit-of-the-stick-inland."

(4.) *Other villages* in Aana have some fragments indicating the origin of their names, such as *Faleasi'u*, "House of the god Siu," who was worshipped there. *Samatau*, "Sacred-on-the-right-side," from a large canoe belonging to the king of Tonga once anchored there, and which, owing to the illness of a lady on board, was made sacred to visitors on the right side. This place was noted for a hero called Poila who once headed the Aana troops, and killed in single combat another hero called Pepe who was the pride of the Tuamasanga, and whose death was the signal for retreat. *Falelatai* and *Faleaseela* trace their names to the children of a couple from Fiji. The one was named Latai, or "Branch-next-the-sea," from his having been born under that part of a large tree. The other was called Seela from another incident in his birth. The one lived on the north side of the mountain, and called the place Falelatai, or "House-of-Latai." The other took the south side, and called his village Faleaseela, or the "House-of-Seela."

(5.) *Lefanga*, or "The bay," is a name embracing a number of villages on the south side of Aana. There is a rising ground there called *Taape*, or "Dispersion," which is said to have been the place where a party broke up and dispersed after a visit to the heavens. There were five Atua men and four belonging to Aana.

As soon as they got up to the skies the people of the god Tangaloa laid a plot to kill them. They prepared a bowl of 'ava for their entertainment, and mixed it with poison, but no one was seriously affected by it. The Tangaloans then prepared a game at sitting in the rain to see who could endure it longest, hoping to kill some of them with cold. One of their party, called Mosofaofulu, that is, "Moso-feather-refuge," covered them with a lot of feathers, and so the rain had no effect on them.

The Tangaloans next proposed a game at floating down a stream which rushed over a cataract, of which strangers were ignorant until they were on the edge of the fall and tumbling over. The visitors were to float first, and Fulufuluitolo, or "Sugar-cane-down," took the lead. He planted his feet firmly on a rock near the fall, and as his party came floating down he seized them one by one and jerked them out of the stream and danger on to the land. And hence the proverb for an unexpected deliverance: "Saved by Fulufuluitolo." It was then the turn of a select party of the Tongaloans to float. Fulufuluitolo held out no helping hand to them, and over the fall they went one after another and were killed.

The Tangaloans next told their visitors they were going to treat them to some food, and made ready accordingly. They plotted at the same time to fall upon them when they were eating and kill them. The Tangaloans went with the food in basket-burdens as usual, carried on poles over the shoulder, and laid all down. The strangers set to work and ate furiously not only the food, but baskets, sticks, and all, to the utter amazement and unnerving of the Tangaloans, who only gaped and stared, and could not summon courage to strike a blow.

As quieter measures failed the Tangaloans proposed a game at club exercise, and thought in that way to kill them off at once. This too was accepted by the strangers. First of all Tangaloaatevalu, "Eight-livered-Tangaloa," or Tangaloa the *plucky*, stepped forward with his club, and up rose Tuimulifanua, "King-of-the-end-of-the-island," club in hand also to fight with him. Every blow was well aimed, struck off a liver, and made Tangaloa reel. By-and-by seven were gone, and as he had only one *pluck* left he called out: "Enough, enough! I am beaten; let me seek something to give you for my life." He went off and brought a fine mat cloth to wear round the body. Tuimulifanua put it round his loins, but it trailed on the ground, and had to be lifted up; hence it was called Lavasii, or "Cloth-lifted-up." He could not be troubled with the long train, and gave

190

it to another of the party called Tuimuaiava, "King-of-the-first-harbour," who kept it and brought it down to the earth. Its name, Lavasii, became a title of chief ruler, and that title has remained in that particular family to this day. One of the Samoans killed in 1876 in a skirmish with the marines of H.M.S. *Barracoutta* had at that time the title of Lavasii.

When the party returned from the heavens they came down on the rising ground referred to at Lefanga, whence they dispersed, and ever since the place has been called Taape, or Dispersion.

CHAPTER XXII.

POLITICAL DIVISIONS AND PLACES OF NOTE ON SAVAII.

There are three principal divisions of Savaii:—

1. THE FAASALELEANGA.—In prose and poetry this part of the island, and even the whole of Savaii, is often called *Sa Lafai*, or sacred to Lafai, and among the legends that chief, Lafai, has an early place. Tupailelei, or Tupai the good, married a daughter of the king of Tonga, and her father ordered that she should go to Tonga some months after her marriage. She started for Tonga, but the canoe was driven by adverse winds to Fiji, and in remembrance of that she called her first child *Vaasiliifiti*, "Canoe drifted to Fiji."

She remained there for a time, but again set out to try and reach her father in Tonga, but again they missed their destination and could only fetch Samoa. As Samoa appeared in the horizon her second child was born, and so she named the girl Samoauafotu, or "Samoa in sight." It was afterwards abbreviated to Safotu. Afterwards they went to Tonga, but again returned to Samoa with Vaasiliifiti, who was now a young man and married. They came with Fotu. When near Savaii they caught a fai or skate, raised it on the mast and made a sail of it, and from that a son of Vaasiliifiti was called Laifai, or "sail made of the fai." After a time they saw a fish nibbling at the fune or core of a bread-fruit, and from that they called another son of Vaasiliifiti Fune or "core." In after-times it was arranged that Lafai was to live in one district, Fune in another, and the aunt Fotu between them to prevent quarrelling. If Lafai commenced strife, Fune and Fotu united to put it down; if Fune took the initiative, then Lafai and Fotu united in restoring peace.

Lafai lived in the place subsequently called Lefaasaleleanga, and divided it into three parts among his three children. Fotulafai occupied the central and leading part. So Talalafai was apportioned Iva on the one side, and Muliangalafai on the other.

When the Tongans were victorious for a time in Samoa they lived on the common at Safotu, and thither the people flocked with food and sundry other articles of tribute to the chief of the invaders, Talaaifeii. Tuna and Fata, two sons of Malietoa Savea, or Malietoa I., went with tribute, but before returning tore up the le'ale'a, or iron-wood mooring-stick to which the Tongan king's canoe was fastened, and took it away, which was alike an insult and a declaration of war. With this they made a club, roused all to battle against the invaders, gained a victory over them, which ended in their leaving, after forming a treaty of peace between Samoa and Tonga, which for upwards of twenty generations of the Malietoa family has remained unbroken. To perpetuate the remembrance of the victory, the Salafai district was called Lele'ale'a, or the "Mooring-stick," and further merged into Faasaleleanga, or "Made sacred to the mooring-stick." When the district after that time united to raise war it was called the lifting of the Le'ale'a club of Malietoa; and all the Faasaleleanga people rose and followed wherever Malietoa and the club preceded.

(1.) *Sapapalii* is the name of the principal settlement of the Malietoa families, and had its origin in one of family heads called Papalii. The celebrated le'ale'a club disappeared about the time when this chief lived, but the deeds and dynasty passed on to posterity.

(2.) *Safotulafai* is the political capital of the Faasaleleanga, and the place where their representative parliamentary gatherings are held, especially in times of war.

(3.) *Iva*, as already referred to, is one of the three divisions of the Faasaleleanga. It is the name of a village to the south of the capital which, with some neighbouring settlements, takes the place in battle of the advance or attacking party. Iva means *tall*. It is said the name originated in a man who undertook to build a house without scaffolding, and from his continued stretching upward added to his stature, and gave a name to the place.

(4.) *Amoa* is the name of a district in a northeasterly direction which protects the capital on that side. Some say its name originated in the fort of the chief Moa which was there during the Tongan invasion; others trace it to a foreign courtship. Of old, they say, the women courted the men, but now it is the reverse. A lady from Fiji called Moa came to seek a husband, and found one in a chief called Nonu, and hence the place was called Amoa, or the settlement of Lady Moa.

2. O LE ITU TAOA, the side of Taoa, was the name of the north side of Savaii. Latterly it has been called *the side of men*, from their bravery in the war against Aana in 1830. But before that it was called the side of Taoa, after a chief of that name of Fijian descent. Tao means a *spear*, and was regarded by the people as an emblem of their heroism as well as their name. When they went to Manono to fight for them in avenging the death of Tamafainga, they laid down a heap of spears in token of their alliance.

(1.) *Saleaula* had its origin in a chief called Aula, of the ancient house of Lafai, who, having distinguished himself in battle, was invited to live there, and take the lead in politics and war; and hence it became the name of the village, and the principal place for public meetings on that side of the island. He had a brother called Tufunga, or *carpenter*, who acted as premier in the Faasaleleanga district.

(2.) *Lealatele*, or "the great road," is the name which embraces a number of villages to the east of Saleaula, and had its name from the ten-mile stretch of level road there.

(3.) Matautu is to the west of Saleaula, and is the district which takes the lead in the attack wherever war is determined on. They trace the origin of the name of their place to Lautalatoa of Fiji, whose son, called Utu, resided there.

(4.) *Safotu* and *Safune* were named after Fotu and Fune, the children of Lafai already referred to. The people of Safune once fought at Faleata on Upolu. Many of them were killed, and the place where their bodies were buried was afterwards called Safune, in remembrance of the slain. Fune had the epithet feai, or *savage*, added to his name, from the habit which he had of biting his finger-nails when he went to battle.

(5.) *Aopo*, a small inland village, was named after a chief called Aopo. It is said that the god Tangaloa of the heavens once gave the people there a choice of two things First, a heap of whales' teeth, or, secondly, a stream of water. They chose the former. The god said, "No; you had better have the water." They still persisted, however, in wishing No. 1, and got it, but it turned out to be a heap of *stones*! They repented and wished the stream, but it was too late. The stream was given to Saleaula, and is called Vaituutuu, or "Given water," to this day.

(6.) *Falealupo*, or the "House for Lupo," is a settlement in the west end of Savaii. A couple from Tonga lived there. They had a son who was lame, and who could only sit on a rock with a fishing-rod and catch small fish called Lupo. They built a house for him there, into which he threw the lupo as he caught them. The god Salevao and his travelling party in passing there one day admired the house, and called it Falealupo, or a house for lupo; and hence the name alike of the fish-house and the settlement.

There were two circular openings among the rocks near the beach at this village, where the souls of the departed were supposed to find an entrance to the world of spirits, away under the ocean, and which they called Pulotu. The chiefs went down the larger of the two, and the common people had the smaller one. They were conveyed thither by a band of spirits who hovered over the house where they died, and took a straight course in the bush westward. There is a stone at the west end of Upolu called "the leaping-stone," from which spirits in their course leaped into the sea, swam to Manono, leaped from a stone on that island again, crossed to Savaii, and went overland to the *Fafâ* at Falealupo, as the entrance to their hades was called. The villagers in that neighbourhood kept the cocoa-nut leaf blinds of their houses all closely shut down after dark, so as to keep out the spirits supposed to be constantly passing to and fro. There was a cocoa-nut tree near the entrance to those lower regions, and this tree was called the tree of Leosia, or the *Watcher*. If a spirit struck against it that soul went back at once to its body. In such a case of restoration from the gates of death the family rejoiced and exclaimed, "He has come back from the tree of the Watcher."

Luaô, or Luaôô, which may be translated "Hollow pit," is another name for the place down which the spirits of the dead were supposed to descend on the death of the body. "May you go rumbling down the hollow pit" was the common language of cursing. At the bottom of this pit, according to the tradition which describes it, there was a running stream which floated the spirits away to Pulotu, the dominions of Saveasiuleo. When they touched the water they were not to look to the right or to the left, or attempt to make for either side. Nor could they come back, as the force of the current rendered that impossible. There was a continued and a promiscuous company of them. Those who had died of various diseases—the good-looking and the unsightly, the little children and the aged, chiefs and common people—all drifted along together. They were, however, little more than alive, and this semi-conscious state continued until they reached the hades of Pulotu, where there was a bathing-place called Vaiola, or "The water of life." Whenever they bathed here all became lively and bright and vigorous. Infirmity of every kind fled away, and even the aged became young again.

It was supposed that in these lower regions there were heavens, earth and sea, fruits and flowers, planting, fishing and cooking, marrying and giving in marriage—all very much as in the world from which they had gone. Their new bodies, however, were singularly volatile, could ascend at night, become luminous sparks or vapour, revisit their former homes and retire again at early dawn to the bush or to the Pulotu hades. These visits were dreaded, as they were supposed to be errands of destruction to the living, especially to any with whom the departed had reason to be angry. By means of presents and penitential confession all injurers were anxious to part on good terms with the dying whom they had ill-used. In one place there was a hadean town called *Noroa*, or Bound, where all the spirits were dumb, and could only "beat their breasts," expressive of their love to one another.

Saveasiuleo, or "Savea of the echo," was the king of these lower regions. The upper part of his body was human, and reclined in a house in company with the chiefs who gathered around him; the lower was piscatorial, and stretched away into the sea. This royal house of assembly was supported by the erect bodies of chiefs who had been of high rank on earth, and who, before they died, anticipated with pride the high pre-eminence of being pillars in the temple of the king of Pulotu.

Falealupo is also strangely associated in Samoan story with Tapuitea, or the planet Venus. Tapu was a man who, with his wife Tea, lived there and had a daughter named Tapuitea, from the union of the names of her parents. The spot on which their house was built they called Leviuli, or "Black apple," from the appearance of the sun one day when covered with a cloud. When Tapuitea grew up she became the wife of the king of Fiji, and went there to live. She had a son, and was wondering one morning what name to give him, when some canoe-builders passed along with their tools rattling in the baskets which they carried over their shoulders. From the rattling of the tools she named her son Toi-va-i-totonu-o-le-ato-a-tufunga, or, as some would write it, Toivaitotonuoleatoatufunga. The formidable polysyllable simply means, "Hatchets rattling inside the baskets of the carpenters." It was abbreviated, however, as in all such cases, and the lad was known by the name of *Toiva*. She had another son, and called him Tasi, which means *one*.

After a time Lady Tapuitea became wild, horns grew out of her head, she ate human flesh, and ten to fifteen Fijians were used up on her cannibal appetite. The king looked aghast when he saw the horns on the head of his wife, went and told Toiva and Tasi that their mother had become a cannibal demon, and that they had better make their escape to Samoa. This they did. Toiva and Tasi were soon missed by their mother. She went about inquiring after them; her husband said he knew not where they were, and after searching all over Fiji she discovered their footprints on the beach in the direction of Samoa. She jumped into the sea, swam to Samoa, and reached Falealupo. She went right into the bush and lived there, but renewed her cannibal indulgences when she could secure a victim. Many of the Falealupo people fled from the place. Tasi became so afraid of his mother that he begged his brother to bury him alive. Toiva did so, and hence the name of a stone there which is called *Tasi*.

One day Tapuitea, on going down from the bush towards the sea, saw the footprints of her son Toiva in the sand, followed them to a pool of water, and there she saw the shadow of Toiva in the water. She was frantic with joy—leaped, and laughed, and screamed, and then tumbled into the pool, clutching in vain the shadow. As she dived her horns struck against a piece of rock and broke off. She was soon on the surface again, however, and Toiva, sitting up in a pandanus tree, called out, "Look up!" She looked up, and there at last was the real body of her missing son. She wept aloud, implored him to come down, and said he had been very unkind to her. He, on the other hand, scolded her, blamed her for the death of all their friends, "and now," said he, "you are going to eat me next." She admitted that she had been cruel, and had been the death of many of the people, but all that was now about to end; she had determined to go up to the heavens, and never again to return. "Go," said he, "go," and away she went. But before going up she promised to shine down as an evening star and give him light for his evening meal. She promised also to give him light in the morning, when he went into the bush at the season of pigeon-catching. Having said this she went up to the heavens, became the planet Venus, which is called Tapuitea. When seen in the morning it is called the Fetu ao, or *morning star*, and is said to have "crossed the heavens." The reason alleged for the star not rising higher was that Tapuitea did not wish to shine higher than the tree on which her son Toiva was accustomed to sit. After she went to the heavens Toiva went and called all the people back from the bush and elsewhere, telling them that his cannibal mother had gone to the heavens, and that there was no further danger to any one. The names of Tasi and Toiva are still perpetuated in family titles at Falealupo.

3. O LE ITU O FAATOAFE, or the side of Faatoafe, was the name of the south side of Savaii; but it is now usually called "the side of *women*," in contradistinction to the north side, which has been named "the side of *men*." The principal political gatherings are held at the bay called *Palauli*, or "Black mud," from the dark mud flats which appear at low water.

Faatoafe, was the name of one of the chiefs of that side of Savaii. He married the daughter of the king of Manua, and resided at Manua for some time. When he was arranging to return to his village on Savaii he requested as a favour, and was presented by the king of Manua with an orator's staff—a long one, reaching to the shoulder, and which the king

199

himself was accustomed to lean upon when addressing public meetings. The king of Manua on handing it to him begged him to speak with it at all the village meeting-places on his way along the coast of Upolu to his residence on Savaii, and exhort the people to "plant the ti-root and sugar-cane, and give up stealing." Faatoafe accepted the staff on those conditions, and was faithful to make "planting and not stealing" the theme of his addresses to the people as he went on from Manua to Savaii.

Faatoafe had a son called Tupai, who ignored his father's teaching, and contrived to be a clever thief as well as a hard worker. He went to a village several miles away on a common errand of begging taro plants. A large contribution was made for him, but, instead of taking them to his own home and plantation, he feigned sickness, and asked permission to plant them there for a time instead of taking them to his own settlement. This was granted, but when the taro was ripe he not only took it all away, but claimed the ground for further use, and kept it ever after.

Near to the place where Faatoafe lived there are two hills, which are said to be the petrified double canoe of *Lata*. Lata came of old from Fiji, was wrecked there, went on shore, and lived on the land still called by his name in the neighbourhood of the settlement of Salailua. He visited Upolu, and built two large canoes at Fangaloa, but died before the deck to unite them had been completed. To Lata is traced the introduction of the large double canoes united by a deck, and which were in use of old in Samoa. Seu i le vaa o Lata, or Seuilevaaolata, "steersman in the canoe of Lata," is a name not yet extinct in Samoa; but the person who bears such a sentential appellation seldom gets more than the first syllable. As in the case referred to, the youth is known and called by the name of Seu.

Salenga is a name which embraces a considerable part of the south-west side of Savaii. Three Fijians came to Samoa, viz. Utu, Taua, and their sister Lenga. Utu took up his abode, as we have already noted, at Matautu. Taua went to a district farther west, now called *Sataua*, and Lenga went to the south-west side, and from her it is still called Salenga. A rock a short distance from the shore was the principal god of the place. An unusually hollow sound, from a change of wind and current, was a call from the god for offerings; and for a time the fish were untouched and sacred to this Samoan Neptune.

A story is told of a chief in this neighbourhood called Ato, who once saved his people from the wrath of Malietoa. Malietoa and his retinue, when on a journey, called at the place, and as usual had a day's entertainment. Some of the people were heard grumbling over the quantity of food necessary for the royal visitors. This was noted, and on reviewing their travels at the end of the journey they decided that the grumbling indignity must be punished. An armed party was selected, and off they went to plunder and burn the settlement, and kill all belonging to the place who fell into their hands. In the midst of the panic which the news of the projected attack threw the people into, the chief Tuato ordered all to be quiet, and do what he told them. He called for cocoa-nut leaves to be plaited, as if for the baking of a pig, lay down on the top of them, told them to enclose his own body in the leaves, sling him on a pole, and carry him and lay him down in that state on the road at the entrance to the village. When the Malietoa troops came up they found, to their astonishment, the chief Tuato done up in leaves and lying across the road all ready to be killed as a sacrifice and put in the oven, to avert the wrath of the king and save the lives of the people. This was sufficient amends to the king. Tuato and the settlement were spared, and his name handed down to posterity as the *saviour* of his people.

Another story is told of a man of this district who had been long on Tutuila, and wished to return to Savaii, but was always refused a passage when a canoe happened to be going. He implored the god Moso to pity and help him. "Come on my back," said Moso; and away Moso went with him, and after a swim of a hundred miles set him down in the evening on the rocks at his own place. "Go and bring me a bunch of cocoa-nuts, that is all I want," said Moso; but the ungrateful man went on shore, and when he got among the houses and the people forgot all about his benefactor, who was waiting patiently for the cocoa-nuts. Moso could bear it no longer, and, when close upon daybreak, went on shore and searched from house to house, feeling for a man whose body had not been freshened by a bath the night before but was rough with saline matter from the ocean. He found him, dragged him away, killed him, and smote at the same time all the people of the place. In the morning they were found dead with their heads on their pillows just as they went to sleep, and hence the phrase "long on the pillow" was used to express *sudden death*.

CPSIA information can be obtained
at www.ICGtesting.com
Printed in the USA
LVHW081909060323
741056LV00004B/53